The Power
—— of a ——
Playing Parent

The Power
—— of a ——
Playing Parent

Engaging and Connecting with our Children

Cara Lynn Jakab

authorHOUSE®

AuthorHouse™
1663 Liberty Drive
Bloomington, IN 47403
www.authorhouse.com
Phone: 1-800-839-8640

Published by AuthorHouse   02/04/2013

ISBN: 978-1-4817-0131-0 (sc)
ISBN: 978-1-4817-0132-7 (e)

Library of Congress Control Number: 2012924280

Any people depicted in stock imagery provided by Thinkstock are models, and such images are being used for illustrative purposes only. Certain stock imagery © Thinkstock.

This book is printed on acid-free paper.

Because of the dynamic nature of the Internet, any web addresses or links contained in this book may have changed since publication and may no longer be valid. The views expressed in this work are solely those of the author and do not necessarily reflect the views of the publisher, and the publisher hereby disclaims any responsibility for them.

Dedication

George: My soul mate and adventure mate! Thank you for choosing me and for being my favorite play companion. You are and always will be my dream man.

Our children Isaiah, Josiah, Bernard and Silvanie: Two born under my heart, two born of my heart. I am humbled to be your mom. I love engaging and connecting with you! Thank you for playing with me!

Clair and Carol Bohlen: My wonderful Dad and Mom. Thank you for being engaging parents; in the past and presently.

The memories endlessly and richly fill my mind and heart.

Grateful

I would first like to humbly thank my precious husband who sweetly encouraged me with this project of turning a 45-minute presentation into a book. You are a man of passion and an amazing husband and father. I am deeply honored to be married to you and to parent our four children with you. I embrace our crazy days and love our crazy adventures. The words, "I love you," and "soul mate" will never say enough! You are the one I prayed for since I was twelve years old.

Thank you to my children for allowing me to talk about our family life in this book. You are four cherished gifts from God. Isaiah, you are an inspiration. Josiah, you are a joy. Bernard, you are big-hearted. Silvanie, you are a sweetie pie. I am so moved that I get to be your mom.

Thank you to the individuals who so timely gave me the confirmation to dive into this project. You know who you are. I appreciate you so much.

Thank you to dear family and friends who encouraged me and prayed for me during the project. Your words were so kind and gracious.

Thank you to the moms who were willing to discuss this important topic over the years and for allowing me to quote you in the book. Our conversations were real and refreshing.

Thank you to Amanda Hall for writing the section on the home-schooling parent. I value your input and I know all of the readers will too.

I want to give a huge thank you to Kathy McKinney for being my editor. God brought us together through our adoption and the impacting ministry of Show Hope. Our family is forever grateful for your hand in this project and your heart in our lives.

I have always been moved by and in awe of the sunset. A daily display of God's splendor. Through God's daily creativity, the front cover idea was born. A special thank you is given to Mike Gazdiewich—our neighbor and friend. Thank you for taking the photo of our hands for the front cover. Watching you take a daily photo of the sunset warms my heart. Your camera communicates deeply and beautifully.

I deeply thank Jim Walters for his amazing insight and his many words of gracious encouragement. You always were just a phone call away. I am humbled that you were so happy to help me with the fine details of this process. Additionally, I want to thank my parents for consistently cheering me on with each and every step of this book. You stayed up late with me as I wrote papers in highschool and college. You are still staying up late with me as I rearrange words. We may be miles away, but we are so close at heart. I love you dearly. Lastly, I want to thank Heidi Olivera for your final edit of this book. You are a mastermind with commas and hyphens. I am honored that you shared your time and talent with me.

Most importantly, I want to thank my Lord, Jesus. For the last two years, every time I gave this talk to a MOPS group, you loudly said to my heart, "Write the book."

Thank you for teaching me to "Live by faith, not by sight." (2 Corinthians 5:7) Thank you for your pursuit of me. I am daily humbled by your love and presence. I am sustained by you and delight in you! You are my greatest treasure. You are my Redeemer and the redeeming quality to each day.

Painted by the Jakab family.
Front cover photo taken by Mike Gazdiewich.

Contents

Praise for the Playing Parent

"Convicting and inspiring all at the same time. Cara Jakab presents a convincing case for connecting to your child's heart through the amazing power of play. How simple is that?

I like to remind parents that when it comes to parenting, the days are long but the years are short. We need to seize those years and we can do it through the power of play. Cara Jakab will show you how.

Read this practical book and then just try it. It works!"

Dr. Tim Kimmel, author of *Grace Based Parenting* and *Little House on the Freeway*

*Psalm 68: 5 "A Father
to the fatherless ...
He sets the lonely in families."*

1

The Power of Play

Two gorgeous pairs of dark chocolate brown eyes stared wide-eyed at me. Their excitement and anticipation filled every ounce of their faces. Their tummies were gratefully full after the very first meal in our home as a family of six.

Pancakes!

Sticky syrup, butter, strawberries and homemade pancakes never seemed quite so special. Three batches and many memory-filled laughs later, we moved from the kitchen into the living room. Now we were peacefully sitting cross-legged on the floor to play a matching game. Bernard and Silvanie were all smiles. They quickly moved from sitting to lying on their stomachs with their feet playfully swaying in the air. They were seemingly so amazed with this quiet and engaged time. Our long moments of eye contact cemented our connection. It was precious play, and they quickly understood the game, even though they didn't understand many English words.

We silently and happily took turns matching plastic Oreo cookies.

Smiles . . . silence . . . It was a surreal and sacred moment as I played with our two long prayed for children. In this memorable moment, they were completely satisfied and I had to pinch myself to make sure this was really happening. The last ten days for these two precious souls could never be fully articulated or understood.

*   *   *

On January 12, 2010, a historical earthquake of unfathomable magnitude devastated the beautiful, but already poverty imprisoned country of Haiti. We had been in the adoption process for two years and had a referral from God's Littlest Angels for our two children, Bernard and Silvanie Exumond. George and I had been to Haiti two times and then took our two boys to the country that we deeply loved to meet our son and daughter in September of 2009.

God's Littlest Angels

John and Dixie Bickel had been ministering to children in Haiti since 1994 and started international adoptions in 1997 through their orphanage. They have always been passionate about the children in their care, and now they were passionate about getting some of these children out of their care. Because of the vast and pressing new needs after the earthquake, they knew that the children who had designated families should go HOME quickly to their forever families!

The World Was Watching

The Bickels were determined to successfully advocate on the children's behalf. Not only were the families of the 81 children watching the tragedy unfold, but the whole world watched with a broken heart for Haiti.

After talking to CNN, NPR, the Today Show, and any other camera or microphone she could get herself in front of, her voice was heard. With her advocacy, along with Mark Udall and other state senators and the work of vital individuals behind the scenes, the Department of Homeland Security sent this life-changing attachment through an e-mail.

"On January 18th, Department of Homeland Security Secretary Janet Napolitano, in coordination with the U.S. Department of State, today announced a humanitarian parole policy allowing orphaned children from Haiti to enter the United States temporarily on an individual basis to ensure that they receive the care they need—as part of the U.S. government's ongoing support of international recovery efforts after last week's earthquake . . . The U.S. Embassy in Port-au-Prince will facilitate their evacuation to the United States so they may be united with their American adoptive parents."

The three page e-mail changed our lives and the lives of many other families all over the U.S. who had to be ready to travel to Miami at a "moment's notice."

"An evacuation to the U.S." . . . Profound words to our ears and hearts!

The anxious and thrilled parents started arriving into the Miami airport at the designated location, Concourse G, in the evening of January 21, 2010. The instruction was to arrive at 4:00 p.m. to receive information and then the children upon their arrival into Miami!

As we arrived, we immediately saw a circle of parents. We joined the widening ring and heard the disappointing, but not surprising news that the plane carrying our precious cargo was still on the tarmac in Haiti. Not having a vehicle to move the plane onto the tarmac, they hadn't been able to leave yet. We hesitantly picked a spot in Concourse G to hang out for a couple of hours with the one couple that we knew from Colorado Springs, Ryan and Naomi Thomas. Grateful for our new friendship, we sat down on the worn carpet by the baggage scale.

All the parents were in good spirits, hopeful and almost giddy that we would be hugging our children before the night was over. Some parents who didn't want to miss out on one ounce of information had been at the airport for a while already and were disappointed about the extended wait. Other parents trickled into Concourse G and heard the initial announcement from other parents. High energy ignited across the room and everyone anticipated their child or children arriving soon!

The Reality of a Reunion

All of the parents had their own pictures in their minds of what the reunion would be like. One can't be two or more years into the adoption process without dreaming of the reunion. During the wait in Concourse G, moms and dads introduced themselves to each other, and a group photo was taken. We came together as strangers, but had one life-changing common denominator — the long Haitian adoption process. We were with people that understood.

We had all completed the same grueling paperwork, had all been evaluated by psychologists to see if we were mentally stable, had all been asked about our family history, how close we were with our mother, father, sisters and how frequently we talked to our mother, father and sisters. We had all been asked about our sex life and how much we weighed. We had all had fingerprints administered at the police department to make certain that we didn't have criminal records and we all had demonstrated the fortitude to jump through the many high-hanging hoops.

Parents stood around and chatted with a sincere camaraderie in their hearts. We all passed the long list of psychological, emotional and physical "tests" and were all sobered at this turn of events in our adoption journeys. We were also sobered at the devastation that now tragically faced the oppressed people in Haiti.

As the first delay of their arrival turned into more delays, parents mingled and then tried to get comfy as we waited for the next update. All of these families had been to Haiti to sign paperwork, so everyone knew that once the plane holding 81 children left Haiti, it would be just 90 minutes until they arrived into Miami and into our arms. People laughed at the stories of needing to be "ready at a moment's notice" to travel to Miami to now be waiting for endless hours. Each family came with its own dramatic story of the last 24 hours; setting up child-care, packing and making travel arrangements were now details to share to pass the time. Everyone also came to Concourse G with a story of where they were in the ten-step Haitian process. The ten-step process was heart-wrenchingly slow. No one could believe the reality of what we were experiencing. We were all skipping steps in this long process for the sake of assisting in the Haitian disaster relief following the earthquake!

At 11:00 p.m., we received the hopeful word that the private plane left Haitian soil. They were on their way! Our babies were in the air and soon would be in our cradled arms. Excitement was rising as moms and dads grasped the grace of God that brought us all there. Not just to Miami, but to the last step of the process. The earthquake brought all of these families to one location to pick up our children and take them HOME! We were unified in spirit as we celebrated the beautiful and miraculous way God works. Only

He can bring a dream out of a nightmare. Only He can bring something beautiful out of such a tragic and devastating earthquake. Only He can bring beauty from ashes.

Isaiah 61:3 "To all who mourn, He will give beauty from ashes; joy instead of mourning; praise instead of heaviness. For God has planted them like strong and graceful oaks for his own glory."

Finally at 12: 37 a.m., they arrived, and several parents took a picture of the arrival board. We had to capture this dramatic and memorable moment. Unfortunately, their arrival into the United States of America on January 22nd brought many more long delays as it was decided that the 81 children should have their photos and finger prints taken before we could see them. And we thought it took a long time to have two adults' finger prints administered.

Try 162 children's hands.

Any of us would have loved to have helped, but that was not allowed. Parents moved from a sitting position in Concourse G into a laying position as we tried to sleep on the floor. As we laid on the floor, many moms joked that we were in labor and I thought, "This is our final wait." It was only appropriate that we all had one last wait.

True to being the life of most parties, my husband added his special humor through the night. The group of people that happened to be within ear shot were graced with George's adoption humor. He was called the stand-up comedian as he joked about the fortitude of the parents. "You do know this is all a test. If you fall asleep during this last test, you won't get your kids." He transitioned from a stand-up comedian to a sit-down comedian and eventually was a lay-down comedian. He didn't disappoint us as his light-hearted humor kept us going all night long.

Throughout the night, some parents walked the halls at the airport to find something to eat, and a few parents were smart and went back to their hotel rooms.

George and I filled the time with writing in our journals, talking to each other and a few other people. We also made frequent calls to our parents to keep them updated. It meant so much to us that they wanted to know every detail to this glorious unfolding.

At 3:00 a.m., George and I gathered some people to pray. Once again, we surrendered the situation to God Almighty. We had endured the grueling months of the adoption process and we needed to endure one last grueling night. We prayed for His strength and mercy. His Presence, as always, was exactly what we needed. He breathed life into our souls.

Finally at 8:30 a.m., the weary and discouraged parents were moved to a conference room. The airport graciously brought all of the parents some food, and we tried to eat a bit.

The hopeful moms and dads who had stayed in amazingly positive spirits all through the night were growing tired of this long wait, and discouragement was high. I would like to call it "failure to progress" in labor and at this point we were hoping for an "emergency C-section" to expedite this seemingly endless wait.

When all hope had seemed lost that we were actually going to be able to take our children out of this airport, we heard the small and angelic voices of 81 children. What? Our children had been moved, and they were now on the other side of the partition wall that separated us. They beautifully and energetically sang songs in Creole. Our children sang, not as if they had been up all night tediously moving through U.S. Customs, but sang with the joy that comes in the morning.

Psalm 30:5 "Mourning may last for the night, but rejoicing comes in the morning!"

Immediately, the conference room held parents with tears streaming down their cheeks. The weary faces who moments before had scowls at the brows were immediately faces that were wet from joy-filled tears.

Now only a wall separated us. Our children were singing for Jesus and they were singing for their parents. Just a little bit longer and we would be able to not just hear their voices, but see their faces.

At 9:30 a.m., Dixie Bickel joined all the parents in the conference room, and she was given a standing ovation. She was every family's hero for providing care for our children and then boldly advocating for them. We all sat in silence as she shared from her heart. Then she started to read from her list. She called not the parents' names, but the names of the children.

The names of the children!

The children!

A life-altering list.

A list that represented a miracle for each child and family involved because it represented 81 children going home!

She started alphabetically by first name, and George and I were thrilled, as Bernard starts with the second letter in the alphabet. Tears started as soon as she called out, "Bernard and Silvanie." George jumped in the air, and I screamed as we ran out of the conference room and into the lobby where Joyce and Molly brought our two children. Joyce Trainer and Molly Little are two of the amazing women who have cared for hundreds of precious children over a decade of serving and living at God's Littlest Angels. We hugged Joyce and Molly so tightly and our hearts longed to sit with them. Since a long list of children was still being called, there was no time. We thanked them from the bottom of our beings. They had loved our children so well and had thoroughly prepared them "to go home to Papa and Mama." Our eyes said more than the time and dramatic situation allowed our mouths to say.

Then they passed us our children. Joyce handed Bernard to George and Molly handed me Silvanie. A dramatic and perfect reunion became our reality. We kissed them and cried with our new children. They hugged us tightly as we gazed into their eyes and touched their cheeks. Together — we were finally together!

We were exhausted and elated — just like labor and delivery. They were in our embrace, where they would always stay!

*   *   *

Just one day later, we were basking in the sweet presence of our adorable new son and daughter in our living room. Once again, I was amazed at the simple power of engaging and connecting through play.

What do you do with brand new family members who have ever-so-dramatically entered your world? How do we set the tone of a connected family after you double your numbers of children over-night? How do you really embrace their presence?

They are home.

Now what?

We play a game, of course!

"You can discover more about a person in an hour of play than in a year of conversation." Plato

2

Amazed by Play

It was not the first time that I was amazed by the power of play.

For ten years, I have spoken to MOPS International (Mothers of Preschoolers) groups on this topic. I have talked to hundreds of moms over the years, and I have always been passionate about playing with our two biological boys—Isaiah, age 13 and Josiah, age 9. Over and over, I have experienced the power it had on the boys' lives and the power it had on my life. Just a few hours in our home and I learned that playing with our two additional children was going to be just as important. They were miraculously home and over two sleepless nights, we were an expanded family!

After our breakfast of champions and after the game of Memory on the floor, the whole family moved to our purple couch and we had a cuddle time with lots of hugs and kisses. As we enjoyed every second together, Josiah said, "It feels like Christmas morning to have them home!" I was amazed by the depth of understanding that Josiah had deep into his soul. Even at age six, he understood the profound gift of his new brother and sister. We were so grateful and in love!

HOME!

FAMILY!

Home! Family!

Simple words, but two words that we would never take for granted!

But how do parents truly make their house a home and foster connection within their family unit? How do families remain close in an intimate relationship with all of the daily realities that vie for our time and attention? How does any family truly become a family?

I know you love your children. This book title would not have caught your eye if you didn't. A book on parenting would not be your choice, if you didn't desire to love your children well.

Stop reading and write down five things that you did for your children today to demonstrate love to them.

_____

_____

_____

_____

_____

Don't think too hard. Have fun with the list!

We love them dearly and deeply. We care for them, we nurture them, we feed them, we taxi them, we clean them, we clothe them, and we teach them.

Yes, we love our children, but parents are busy all day and every day. Sometimes from morning until night, we methodically cross tasks off of our long to-do lists. Or we work all day and our many responsibilities loudly await us as we walk into our evening at home.

Daily life makes it hard for us to sit down and engage with our children because of its maintenance and the sometimes frantic pace that we choose to live our days.

What is the result?

The result is really quite tragic and causes more hurts and rejections than sometimes we ever accept or realize. The result is that we often say to our children,

"I will play with you later."

"I will paint your fingernails later."

"We can play a game later."

"I will toss the football with you later."

"I will read to you later."

The result is that we can be with our children day after day, but not connect with them.

The sad and harsh reality is that "the later" sometimes or even rarely comes. Our kids are waiting for the "later."

We don't give them true time in our day and then one day they don't really want to give us the time of day.

When my oldest son, Isaiah, was two years old, I have a specific memory of him learning to play "Hide and Seek." I was so excited about this game because it was something new we could play together. We both thoroughly enjoyed this newly discovered playtime. While we were chasing through the house playing "Hide and Seek," I started something that I liked to call "Creative Housekeeping."

Armored with a rag and Windex in my back pocket and a plan of attack in my mind, when it was my turn to hide, I chose a place that I knew needed to be cleaned. For instance, I would hide in the coat closet.

Then, while Isaiah was sweetly counting and then enthusiastically seeking, I would straighten the shoes and hang the coats that for some odd reason had lost the battle with gravity and had never made it to the hanger. Then during my next round of "hiding," I ducked in the shower to clean down the tub and walls. Do you know how much you can get done in those coveted 60 seconds? When it was my turn to "seek" for my precious son, I would pick up some toys strewn on the floor or throw some dirty towels down the laundry chute.

I couldn't have been more thrilled. He loved the game, and I loved it, too. To this day, I don't know if he ever knew I was multi-tasking, so it really worked out for both of us. There were happy hearts all around.

Multi-tasking is valuable. It has a place. Every parent needs to multi-task at certain times of the day, and we can be somewhat successful at it.

But it was during one of those Creative Housekeeping Episodes that I was convinced that my son deserved and needed a time in each day when I was not multi-tasking. A time in the day when I was not playing and talking on the phone. A time in the day when I was not focused on a game and a task simultaneously. He needed a time in the day when I was truly engaged with him, sitting down, and looking into his eyes as we play.

That Creative Housekeeping conviction was eleven years ago, and it changed my life and the way that I parent! Now the number of children in our home is four, and the ages range from four years old to thirteen years old. To this day, I love straightening up a closet or clearing out dust bunnies on the hardwood floor when I play Hide and Seek with the kids. However, I also have made engaging with my children one of my highest priorities in my day and week.

Why did my son, Josiah, say that it felt like Christmas morning during Bernard's and Silvanie's first morning in our home? I know he understood the gift of their arrival, but I am confident that it went deeper than that. We weren't opening gifts. What elements reminded him of Christmas?

Just like that treasured first morning with our new additions, one highlight of Christmas morning is that it is a time when the focus is the family. Everyone is home! Technology is turned off. Parents don't answer the phone on Christmas morning. Laundry is not folded, bills are not paid. Tasks are not the focus. The focus on the morning that we celebrate Jesus' birth is making meaningful family connections and new memories. Time beautifully stops, and loved ones are fully content to just be together.

Do we really need to wait for Christmas morning to have an engaged time with our children? It would be ridiculous to say "yes." However, how often do we truly set everything aside to engage with the children that we so dearly love? Just like a pastor once said, "Give me your checkbook, and I can tell you what your priorities are." I'd like to say, "Give me your smart phone, and I can tell you what your priorities are." Are we really making connecting and engaging with our children a top priority during the week? How do we do that, anyway?

I strongly feel that one way that connection comes is through sitting down and playing. Even with a heart of passion for play, I too struggle! Since it is a daily battle to make it a reality, for years I have explored this topic. I desired to discover ways that parents could be more intentional and heighten our awareness of how many times we say, "Later — I will play with you later." But even more importantly, why do we say "later?" There is always a reason that we tell our children, "I can't play with you, but I will later." What if we could be more aware of the preventers of play?

That is my heart's desire. I want to be aware of my Preventers. My hope is that as you read the next chapters you will become aware of your Preventers, as well.

Throughout this book, I am going to share the importance and value of playing with our children. I will be sharing seven Preventers of Play and seven Powers of Play.

A few important notes before we begin our adventure of connecting with our kids:

1. I do know that some parents don't struggle with playing with their kids and it is their strength in parenting. The next chapters can still be an inspiration to you. You will be encouraged to keep on doing what you are doing and will be reminded of the powerful way that you are parenting your child or children. However, after interviewing, exploring and speaking on this topic for so many years, I know that the majority of parents do struggle.

2. This book **is not** about being a stay home mom, stay home dad, working a home-based business, or working outside the home part time or full time. You have made choices that you feel are best for your family. This book is about a much more important topic. This book is about fully engaging with our children when we are with our children. It is about making our connection with them a true reality and top priority.

3. Over the years that I have presented this topic, I have had a few moms talk to me about their concern that children will grow up thinking that the parents' job is to entertain them all day. This book is not about mindlessly appeasing them all day. This book is about intentionally engaging with our children.

4. If you are a parent of a 16-year-old, don't put the book down to collect dust. This book is for parents who have children from 16 hours old to 16 years old, or really any age when you get right down to the facts.

5. A very common response from moms is "I don't play with my kids. My husband does that job." I would challenge moms to keep reading. You can be a playing and connecting parent, too.

As you read, please personalize this topic. Which Preventer is your personal struggle? Each chapter is written with a Preventer of Play and then the correlating Power of Play. Each chapter will heighten your awareness of your specific struggle and the powerful way that we can overcome that struggle. If you frequently say "no" to the familiar and sometimes dreaded question, "Will you play with me?" **there** is a deeper reason!

Let's explore the deeper reasons, so that our "no" can become a joyous "yes" more frequently. Join me as we explore the power of play in our children's lives and the power of play in our lives as parents.

Your children will be so happy that you did and so will you!

"There are no seven wonders of the world in the eyes of a child. There are seven million." Walt Streightiff

3

Preventer #1-Too Messy

It was a gloriously quiet moment. The boys were at school, and Silvanie was watching T.V. It was Wednesday. At our house, that meant "Watching Wednesday." We allow the kids to watch selected T.V. on Wednesdays. They look forward to this time and so do I. It is always a much needed time to regroup and cross something off of my "list."

On this Wednesday, I decided to enjoy my personal and quiet moments in the sunroom. This space is one of my favorite places in our home. With prayer journal in hand, I sat down on the couch that we victoriously found at a used furniture store. I gazed out all of the windows that encased the room. I breathed in the silence. I prayed, "Thank you God, for your sweet presence, your never-ending love. Thank you for the birds singing, flowers blooming, sun shining, grass greening, children schooling, sky humbling, mountains declaring. I take in your Spirit and pour out gratefulness."

From the rising of the sun to the going down of the same, the Lord is my life-line in daily life. Our time together restores me over and over again, and His love is new every morning. I didn't want this quiet to end. As I gazed outside into the beautiful outdoors, my gaze moved inside and abruptly the beauty stopped. This is what I saw on the floor:

A blanket thrown on the floor — why couldn't the user fold it and put it back where they found it?

An art project of paint and brushes that we used the day before. Because it didn't get put away, some of the brushes were dried!

A soccer ball that never made it to the ball bucket that sits just inches away.

An Easter basket that now had Easter grass strewn all over the place. (Note to self! I hate Easter grass. Don't ever buy it again!) Easter was ten days before. Why were the Easter baskets still out anyway? I would be finding Easter grass in the nooks and crannies of the house for months.

A plastic birthday tablecloth that was waiting for someone to wipe it down a few times before folding it up, putting it away in the birthday supplies to be ready to reuse for the next birthday. That "someone" would probably be me, but I was hoping that the person that spilled the juice would be the one to wash it. I just needed a minute to follow through with that.

A doll that had been played with outside that now had grass matted and stuck in her hair. We needed a "hair dresser" to take out the grass before we could take the doll back inside.

Let's face the hard cold facts! Family life is messy! I love a clean sun room and love a clean house. We daily strive for Jakab team work that allows the house to be and stay clean. But the reality is that days can start and finish with an overwhelming mess on our hands!

One particular early morning, before I crawled out of bed I talked with Jesus for few minutes. I laid in bed praying. "Help me to be strong, firm and steadfast and may this day be a gift back to you." I needed Jesus that day and every day!

Before I made it too far down the hall and into the morning, a mess awaited me. One child had taken off her nighttime diaper, and it lay open right on the bedroom floor. The next child jumped out of the top bunk with his sleepy eyes and footie pajamas. Innocently, he stepped right into the messy diaper. The mess was all over his pajamas and now the floor. Out came the bleach and a wide-eyed mother to mop the hardwood floor and start a load of soiled laundry.

The adventure and messes continued at breakfast while getting ready for school. Not one, not two, but three cereal bowls were spilled. Out came the wide-eyed mother again to mop the kitchen floor. I encouraged the kids to join me on the floor, since this time the cleanup was a bit more kid friendly. The kids joined me in mopping and they also joined me in inhaling and exhaling a big sigh. All of these messes happened back to back, and it was not even 7:30 in the morning. In my mind I said, "Oh Mama, put your game face on. This is going to be one of those days!"

Yes, messes are reality each day.

One child kept adding flour, flour and more flour to the homemade pizza dough when I stepped out of the kitchen for a minute while making supper. So, there was flour all over the kitchen.

One child secretly ordered apps on Isaiah's Kindle Fire.

Two children tracked mud from their boots all over the house after playing "Puss and Boots."

In some form, messes are all around. So, we tirelessly try to stay on top of the messes; paperwork, laundry, school work, school supplies and proof of our child's efforts of excellence at school. There are also, groceries, meal prep and dishes. We have messes from work and volunteer responsibilities. Maybe even a mess of some home-improvement project. What mess is around you at this moment? Look around, what awaits you when you put this book down?

Many days, we are up to our wrinkled foreheads in messes and the thought of pulling a game off of the shelf or creating a new artistic masterpiece with glue and glitter is just one more mess that we can't even deal with right now.

One mom that I recently talked to said, "If I don't stay focused on preventing the messes, today's messes will become tomorrow's messes and then we are all overwhelmed and cranky."

I can relate. Just yesterday I heard myself saying, "We are not playing that game. Do not get it out. We have enough messes going on right now."

How sad is that? Very sad if that is our family's reality day after day. Do we push our kids and their desires to engage with us aside because they are just too messy?

Power #1

The Power of Memories

If your biggest challenge when playing with your kids is the mess, then contemplate the Power of Memories.

Summertime always fosters many rich memories. I love summer and having the kids home: playing family softball, extended games of Monopoly, playing at the pool together, playing Dominoes or Charades around the campfire. In addition, hiking, family rock climbing and visiting as many parks as we can are always favorites.

One highlight has been our family team efforts that over the years grew into a fundraiser. One summer years ago, Isaiah and baby Josiah created their summer lemonade stand. We loved seeing and serving our neighbors with a glass of summer-time iced lemonade. The very next summer, the words written on our family made poster were no longer advertising a lemonade stand, but an ice cream stand as we sold ice cream sandwiches and Drumsticks. Once again, we loved seeing our sweet neighbors and serving them a fun cold treat. While we waited for the next customers to drive by, we loved sitting together and playing a game in the shade.

When the school days came to an end, the boys were excited for a new summer creation; the following summer, they made a backyard carnival complete with games, a snack shop by mom and a prize booth made by Isaiah.

This child-inspired progression of projects continued, and the ultimate adventure was born with Carr St. Café in 2009. For three summers, we've had a little fund raising café at our house that sits on Carr St. Together, we grocery shopped for the event, chose a charity, planned the food that we wanted to serve and had a family prayer time before "customers" started arriving. We had a cute laminated menu, centerpieces, and each child had an important role as we loved serving lunch to friends and neighbors. In 2011, we served lunch to 60 people. Humbly and gratefully, we were able to raise $931 for the amazing ministry, Mission of Hope—Haiti!

Mission of Hope was founded in 1998. For years, they have daily served Haiti by meeting the physical and spiritual needs of the Haitian population. They have a desire to serve this beautiful nation and see lives changed and empower future generations through education, church advancement, orphan care, agriculture and independent living initiatives. Their passion is to set people free from the prison of poverty. For more information on this effective and life-changing ministry, you can visit their website at Mission of Hope — Haiti. You will be in awe!

During Carr St. Café, the boys and I looked at each other a few times to confirm that we were crazy, and at the end of the two days we all collapsed together on the couches. Our bodies and minds were exhausted, but our tanks were full with our purposeful togetherness.

Is our Carr St. Café a big mess? Oh my, yes! Our family fundraiser produces the biggest **mess** ever! If dear friends hadn't stayed to help wash dishes, it would have taken me three days to clean up from the aftermath. But the event also fosters one of our family's strongest **memories**. During Carr St. Café, the family playtime was really quite a lot of work. Work and play can seamlessly join together, as the family is unified in efforts and spirit.

When we placed our house on the market in 2011, the kids' biggest concern was the name of the new street where we would live. What would we call our new Café? "Carr St. Café" had such a ring to it.

The very day we moved into our new house on 34th Drive, the kids discussed the name of our new café. This year, our 65 guests came to 34 Bistro. We were honored to raise $1,400 for our beloved orphanage, God's Littlest Angels. Over a turkey avocado sandwich or grilled chicken pasta salad, our friends and neighbors watched a short video about the precious orphanage.

A pile of dishes later, we celebrated the mess. The mess was filled with memories and, most importantly, money going to Haiti.

An older mom who had grown children expressed, "These days my house is always clean and quiet. I much prefer the mess and noise."

Who said we had to have a clean house every day? Who said that? Believe me, we like order in our home and we are teaching our children work and responsibility. But my expectations of what order looks like in our home will match my priorities. Order and cleanliness will not be at the cost of disengaging with my children. Cleanliness is not next to godliness.

It is okay to go to bed with dishes in your sink because you read to your children instead. It is okay to go outside and play with your kids in the backyard while the dust settles into another layer on your furniture. It is okay; we'll get to the dust soon enough!

This very familiar poem is a necessary reminder for parents while we are in the trenches of our daily messes.

<u>One Hundred Years From Now</u>

(excerpt from "Within My Power" by Forest Witcraft)

One hundred years from now

It won't matter

What kind of house I lived in

How much money I had in the bank

Nor what my clothes looked like

But

The world may be a little better

Because, I was important

In the life of a child.

I would like to add a second verse. I'd like to join Forest Witcraft in his heart for children.

<u>One Hundred Years From Now</u>

One hundred years from now

It won't matter

How clean was the house I lived in

How much I mopped our hardwood floors

Nor what my silverware drawer looked like

But

The world may be a little better

Because I was important

In the life of <u>MY</u> child.

Our children need us to engage with them. Sometimes engaging is messy. But the mess will bring a memory for sure.

After my refreshing and renewing quiet moments in the sunroom on that Watching Wednesday, instead of letting the blanket, art project, and other items that made a mess enrage me, I wrote down this list in my journal.

A blanket that cuddled

A painting project that engaged mother and children

A soccer ball that challenged father and sons

Easter basket that rejoiced

Birthday tablecloth that celebrated

A doll that loved

I choose not to see the mess. I choose to see memories. I choose to see life abundant!

"That's the real trouble with the world, too many people grow up." Walt Disney

4

Preventer #2
Too Boring

I asked hundreds of moms, "Why is it hard to sit down and play with your child?" Many moms said that they just don't like it and are rarely in the mood. One mother who I spoke to worked full time at a family-owned business. At the time of the interview, she was 35 and had two boys, ages four and seven. She said, "It is hard to sit down and play with my children because I just don't enjoy it. It is so boring."

I so appreciated her honesty. That is exactly how many parents feel. Playing with their kids is not something they naturally enjoy; therefore, they don't do it. We often don't engage in activities that we don't enjoy. Unfortunately, if we view engaging with our children as boring, then our children are set aside while more enjoyable activities take a higher priority in our days.

Bor-ing

1. Uninteresting: stimulating no interest or enthusiasm, dull, dreary.

Is hanging out with our children dull and dreary? Does connecting with our children truly not stimulate any interest or enthusiasm? Unfortunately, sometimes it is the heartfelt truth.

A father recently said to me, "I struggled with playing with my kids because it just didn't interest me." He had a challenging time connecting with his children when they were little. Now that his kids are older, they have moved into a bonding season with bike rides and family games of golf.

Power #2

Power of Learning

You might say to me, "playing with my child is too boring for me," but listen: this is how you enter their world and connect with their soul. It is also extremely motivating to know the vast amount of learning that occurs simply through your play together.

During game time, your children learn to recognize colors, shapes and letter recognition. They learn to read as they recognize words that they see often and they are exposed to meaningful print as you read the directions together. They learn how to count, as well as learn number recognition in games like Candy Land. They learn to add as they count dice in games like Parcheesi or Yahtzee. They also learn to take turns, complete a task, how to problem solve and how to gracefully win and how to gracefully lose. Further, they learn fine motor skills in games like HI HO! Cherry-O.

During pretend play, children learn communication, sequencing, and creativity. In addition, play promotes their imagination and language skills.

During outside play, they learn ball skills and gross motor skills.

The former teacher in me could go on and on about the growth and development of a child during playtime. It is absolutely phenomenal! Their hearts, minds, and bodies all develop with a little sit down playtime or active play.

Karyn Purvis, Ph.D., director of Texas Christian University's Institute of Child Development, whose heart's cry is connecting with our children, stated in her book, *The Connected Child*, "Play is shared joy and a great vehicle for active learning."

One mom who I spoke to about playing with her children said, "There are so many opportunities to teach them in play. So much learning that happens. Watching my son and daughter play, I know that my son is teaching my daughter ways to play that he learned when I played with him."

When I taught at an elementary school, I could tell which students had playing parents. These students had acquired basic and foundational learning that is often gained during play.

A mother of two children who were one and two years old at the time of my interview said, "One benefit that I have experienced from playing with my son is that he learns how to play. He is actually learning about toys and not just breaking them."

I love that comment. Simply learning about toys! Too often a parent says, "Go play" or, "Go on now, go play." Sometimes, our children truly don't know how to "Go play!" When we sit and engage with them, they learn how to play.

I have been giving a presentation on this topic for years and continue to be convinced every time I speak about the value of teaching our children how to play. When I taught Isaiah and Josiah how to play a new card game and then watched them play the game together later in the day, my mother's heart was overjoyed. Playing Ladder Ball with the boys in the backyard and then observing them from the kitchen window play two more rounds while I made dinner was a simple satisfaction that I never took for granted.

The delight of teaching our kids how to play rose to a very new dimension when Bernard and Silvanie entered our world. We experienced the curious and destructive hands of our two angels who had lived in an orphanage for ten months. After spending time in six orphanages in Haiti, we observed that children in a Haitian orphanage do not know how to show respect for toys or personal items. Small children living in orphanages throw toys, bang them on the ground, and throw them off the balcony. They don't understand the idea of ownership. This is a concept that needs to be taught.

When the kids first came home, they broke so many household items and toys that belonged to the older boys. It was extremely frustrating to us all and overwhelming to redirect their tendency to chew and break items. We truly had to teach them how to play with toys because breaking the toys is what came naturally. Many children play with toys beyond and outside their intended use. However, Bernard's and Silvanie's natural tendency went way deeper than just thinking outside the typical box with a certain toy. Destruction was a harsh reality of their early behavior. For quite some time, our sad motto was, "If it can get broken, it will get broken."

But play is powerful, and it has been a season of grateful growth.

I am confident that watching your child learn is exciting to you. Many parents feel that promoting their child's growth and development is one of the profound joys of being a father or mother. If you struggle with the Preventer: Too Boring, then the Power of Learning can dramatically motivate, excite, and inspire you to sit down and play.

Focus on specific areas of learning and play. If your child is four years old and needs to learn numbers, play Skip-Bo. If your child is eight and needs to learn how to count money, pull out a few food cans and reused grocery bags and play grocery store. If your child is twelve and needs to learn how to communicate without saying "like" three times in every sentence, then take turns performing a skit.

Focus on your child's learning stage and play, play, play!

Jesus said, "Come to me all who are weary and burdened and I will give you rest." Matthew 11:28

5

Preventer #3
Too Tired

Pleasant clouds drifted across the May sky. The end of the year activities for the three boys were winding down, and I was downright exhausted. Some weeks were so full during the school year that it sent my mind spinning. On that particular afternoon, Isaiah was with friends and I took the three younger kids, plus one friend for Josiah, to the neighborhood park to play.

We tumbled out of the floor-cluttered van. In my right hand was my cell phone. In my left hand were a pencil and my day-timer. Just having a few minutes to write and coordinate the details of the last ten days of school would be so helpful and restful. I was ready to make a few phone calls to iron out a few logistics of the rest of the week and my day-timer was calling me. I love spending time with my day-timer. It makes me feel organized. It calms my spirit and rests my mind.

My heart started beating faster with excitement that I might actually be able to sit down with my important tools for a moment. Josiah must have seen me settling in at the picnic table because he quickly yelled, "Mom, come on. Let's play!"

Without a care in the world, my three kids and their friend ran to the sand pit. I had an instant agonizing pull. Rest or play. Play or rest. I gazed at the four adorable children in the sand pit. I gazed at my adorable cell phone and day-timer. (You can see that I am not a tech savvy mama because I still love my day-timer!)

What should I do? The adorable kids won, and I ran to the back of the van that was parked close by to grab some plastic cups left over from our soccer party. I joined the kids with brightly colored plastic cups in hand!

They were thrilled with my arrival and the passing out of the tools that I found. We had a grand time as we played in the sand — building and shaking. We each took turns trying to form the best castle. We mixed sand and water. A little more sand, a little more water. Some castles fell into a big pile of wet sand with groans from us all. Some castles successfully came out of the orange and green cups with cheers from us all.

Digging our fingers into the wet sand was therapeutic. The kids left their anxiety from the school day deep in the sand. I left the anxiety of my day deep in the sand. Sand under our fingernails confirmed a fun time was had by all. As we made castles, I was so grateful that I seized the moment "to play."

The Castle Connection was refreshing and restful!

Parenting is exhausting. Because of our cluttered and complicated lives, many days we have to dig deep to parent well! So now my new motto is:

Dig deep

Dig deep — deep into the sand and play. Get the sand under your fingernails and play!

If "Too Tired" is the preventer that keeps you from playing with your children, then the Power of Rest will heal your tired body and soul.

Power #3

The Power of Rest

Frigid night air breathed frost over our windows in January. I was completely wiped out from the week and was deeply experiencing the post-holiday exhaustion. I didn't even have enough energy to make it to the weekend. In a couple of weeks, we were going to be gratefully celebrating the one-year anniversary of Bernard's and Silvanie's homecoming. However, at the moment, I was quite overwhelmed with our sweet four! Thankfully, I mustered enough strength to make dinner. After our family meal, it was Isaiah's night to wash the dishes and for that I was very grateful. Is 6:30 p.m. too early to go to bed? As I went to Bernard and Silvanie's bedroom to tidy up, I encouraged the three younger kids to join me for a five-minute Room Rescue. With helping hands all around, we whipped the room into shape.

Then I succumbed to the welcoming bottom bunk and quietly pulled the covers up to my chin. Instead of being sad that mom was disengaging, Bernard started combing my hair with a comb that had been on the floor. Without missing a beat, Josiah and Silvanie started massaging my feet.

Did I really look that weary? How did my kids know I needed some rest? Maybe it was the ponytail that had been in my hair for three straight days. After a bit of precious time, Josiah added a new idea to my brand new favorite playtime.

"Now we are on a ship and you are the queen of Haiti. I am a Ninja to protect you and to protect Haiti." Bernard enthusiastically joined Josiah's new Ninja idea and closely watched all of Josiah's smooth moves before he added his own new Ninja twists. Silvanie took over the combing of my hair, and I was one small beautiful step away from sleep. While I soaked in the relaxing playtime, the noise-making Ninjas fought off any and all threats to the ladies on the ship. Lying on the bed, even with kids and Ninja noises all around me, was restful and refreshing — refreshing for the shipmates and the Ninjas. I loved the pampering reminder that even when we have the "mommy meltdowns" or "daddy disasters," we can still be intentional to engage and connect.

The time was also refreshing for the Ninjas as they had my full attention. Well, maybe not full attention since I was almost asleep! But they graciously appreciated my humble efforts and my "queen comments" now and then. Later that night, we all went to bed with full tanks from our playtime and a new memory of our togetherness! I went to bed with beautifully combed hair and lotion-covered feet! I think we all went to sleep with smiles upon our faces.

What would happen to the souls of our children if parents viewed the time with their children as truly restful? What if we set aside the notion that playing with our children is tiring and exhausting?

I want my perspective of playtime with my children as the time in my day that I get to actually sit down and rest. I want to view playtime with my children as my break.

Our scurried schedules cause true exhaustion. It is a harsh reality of parenting in our culture. The speed of our day and our wide range of responsibilities keep us running at a head-spinning speed; we drop into bed at the end of another day.

Tim Kimmel, in his profound book, *Little House on the Freeway,* focuses on the crucial need for rest. "In the midst of the most hurried and haggard schedule, families can discover a lasting calm that reaches into the very center of our lives . . . We can experience an internal rest that bathes the soul in contentment."

Rest provides more than we realize or sometimes can articulate as it seamlessly produces contentment and calm in the middle of chaos. These are necessary ingredients in life for every member in the household.

When your children pursue you in play, do you think, "I am too tired. I just can't"?

If the weight of your eyelids is all you can focus on this evening, maybe you can't run around and play Frisbee at the park. Or you might not have enough energy to shoot hoops in the driveway or bust out your best moves during a dance party, but you could engage in a slow-paced activity to rest a bit together!

Maybe you could play "Hair Salon" or take turns giving foot massages, color at the table, or paint a picture outside. You could even play house. Sit down and direct the "household."

I have a friend with three kids, who suffered from mononucleosis. She was in bed for weeks. Guess what time of year it was? Summer, of course! However, she fondly remembers that season as a time when they all cuddled up and read, inside, outside and upside down all summer long.

Rest—true rest. It can be a reality and priority as we experience calm in the chaos of our cluttered lives. All parents need rest and so do our kids! They need calm in their hearts. They need calm for their minds.

Our family unit needs rest, and our daily playtime can wonderfully and naturally provide genuine rest.

Setting aside time to connect with our kids sends us into a place of sanity and serenity amidst the insanity. Serenity and sanity . . . I'll take a cup of that each day.

One night after an active story time, I walked through the kitchen and grabbed an empty egg carton that had been sitting on the counter from when I emptied the 18 eggs into their tray in the fridge. Along with the egg carton, I also grabbed a handful of pennies from their spot in the drawer.

"Come on guys. We are going to play a game," I said. Bernard pumped his arm and energetically said, "Yes." I explained the mom made-up game, and they were thrilled. Everyone took a turn throwing a penny into the egg carton and saying what they were thankful for about the day.

Our game of thanksgiving was so simple. Our game of thanksgiving was so fun. There were so many smiles with our hearts of thanksgiving. I knew we'd be using the grateful egg carton again. Maybe I would decorate it and make a cute title to go on the top of the carton. Maybe I would leave it just the way it was.

Time ticked and it was time for bed.

One by one, they gave me a hug as they passed by me before heading to their room of rest. Bernard stopped and said, "Thanks for the game Mom, you are a lovely girl. I could hug you all day."

Stop, rest and play!

They can all go together in a very beautiful and powerful way, even with just an egg carton, a handful of pennies and a heart of gratitude.

"If you haven't time to respond to a tug at your pants leg, your schedule is too crowded." Robert Brault

6

Preventer #4
Too Busy

Have you ever noticed that when you ask anyone how they are doing, the majority of answers are "We are so busy"?

"How has your week been?"

"How was your day?"

The answer is always "busy!"

Sometimes even with a huge and helpless sigh, we declare we are so busy.

What has happened in our society that causes most people to describe their life as "busy"? We do live in a fast-paced society, and it seems almost impossible to avoid the fast pace. We have days packed full and we simply don't have time. Playing with our kids is the last thing on our mind and often not on our "to-do" list.

Tim Kimmel openly discusses the marks of a hurried home and says our society has a "love affair with haste."He very poignantly states, "We call it convenience and there is no doubt that many of our modern conveniences have made some of the mundane duties of life more tolerable. But there is a subtle programming that goes on at the same time. It's not long before we drive our lives the same way we drive our cars — too fast."

Do we have a love affair with haste? Do we love our busy schedules?

Our homes and therefore our hearts are hurried. Dr Kimmel continues, "It's funny how easily we can find ourselves in a fast-forward mindset. It doesn't require a conscious effort. Actually, it is the logical outcome of the forces surrounding us each day."

We have to ask ourselves if we are "fast-lane parents?" Because our culture values a "hurried home," we have to diligently and actively counter against this mindset. If we don't, our children will grow up with the same theory — Busy is better.

According to Karyn Purvis, author of *The Connected Child,* many families live at breakneck speed. They hurry to work, to daycare, to civic meetings, and to social engagements. They ferry the kids from scouts to soccer to piano lessons to school and back again.

The parent becomes a chauffeur with a checkbook, someone who waves goodbye in the morning and barely says hello again at night." (Karyn Purvis in *The Connected Child*)

A 30-year-old stay-at-home mom of a five year old and a three year old admitted, "One of the hardest things about playing is my busyness." This darling mom was away from home a lot with preschool, exercise group, mom's group, play group and volunteering in a few places. She was the classic stay-at-home mom who was never home.

Our busyness easily prevents us from truly engaging with our children, and days can go by without a sincere parent and child connection. Sadly, the popular Veggie Tale ditty can eloquently describe our parenting style and daily reality.

"Busy, busy dreadfully busy. You've no idea, what I have to do. Busy, busy, shockingly busy. Much much too busy for you."

In this favorite Veggie Tale story, three individuals who are filled with importance and status are much too busy to help a man in need. Even though the man lies on the ground completely dependent upon someone stopping long enough to notice him, they pass by. All three busy people make the choice not to engage.

Tragically, sometimes we are parents filled with importance and status.

We choose to pass by our children in need as they play in the backyard or play on the computer. They are dependent upon someone noticing that they had a hurtful day or heavy heart. Sadly, we make the choice to not engage.

Do we schedule our hectic day and set up our lives in such a way that we are truly too busy to engage with our children? Do we really expect our children to build their own character traits, learn important life lessons, and pursue their own goals and dreams?

Do we really expect our children to feel connected to us as we masterfully whip through yet another week?

Do we truly expect them to just follow a few steps behind our hurried cadence?

Playtime has become a gauge for me. It is my indicator if I have made my day too busy. If a couple of days go by and I haven't intentionally engaged with my children, then I have allowed my days to be too busy.

Power #4

Power of Balance

I have always strongly disliked answering the question, "How are you?" with the common word, "busy." I don't want the "B" word to be the word I use to describe my life or my family's life. Four kids or not, I have higher hopes than "busy."

One day, I made my frequent trip to a local thrift store to shop for a pair of size two tennis shoes for Bernard. As I passed a bookshelf, I saw the book title on the second shelf that ignited a cartwheel from me. The book that inspired the "almost cartwheel moment" was *Busy But Balanced* by Mimi Doe. She discusses practical and inspirational ways to create a calmer, closer family. Because I care so much about balancing the busy lifestyle, this book jumped out at me.

Are there really ways that we can balance our jammed packed days?

I would like to say a victorious "yes!"

If your main preventer of engaging with your children is your busyness, then the power of balance will bring peace to your soul and schedule.

Balance is such a popular word, and you may feel even a little annoyed because it is overused, but it is still a needed reminder for parents.

I'd like to share about balance with my dining room table. My dining room table is sometimes filled with soccer schedules, bills, laundry, volunteer folders, a new recipe for our dinner that I am making for friends, church responsibilities, "thank you" notes that need to be written from the most recent birthday and paint swatches waiting to be the color chosen for the family room. My dining room table is the indicator if I have made my day or week too busy.

Is parenting the next generation busy? Absolutely!

But do we sometimes add too many other activities to our dining room table, day-timers, and smart phones? Why do we add so many activities to our days?

That answer would take a little self evaluation: necessary reflection of our rush and running.

Sometimes we are running from people that are less than three feet high. We would rather be busy than hang out with our kids all day. Sometimes we are running from the mundane jobs at home that are never complete. Or maybe you're at your place of employment for 50 hours a week and more work awaits you the second that you drop your keys on the counter. Sometimes we fall into the deadly trap that our kids "have to be" involved in ALL activities for their future to be merry, bright and successful.

Why is your family life so busy? What comes to your mind? Spend a few minutes writing your thoughts.

_____

_____

_____

_____

_____

One day, I felt particularly busy. During that season, we had two sons. They were involved with a quiet activity, and I was busy with my day's agenda. Isaiah came to my side and said, "Mom, will you play with me?"

My first mental response was, "Don't you see I am busy?"

Thankfully, I said, "Yes, what do you want to play?"

Enthusiastically and without hesitation he answered, "Doctor."

We pulled out all of the needed items that every top-notch doctor needs: clipboard, stethoscope, thermometer, insurance cards, co-pays and surgery scrubs. We happily took turns being the doctor and the patient. We creatively thought of our answer to the doctor's question, "What are we seeing you for today?"

After taking turns for about 30 minutes, Isaiah was the doctor and he confidently said, "Ma'am, I am sorry, but we have an emergency in the nursery." (He was referring to Josiah who had been laid down for a nap). In his precious doctor's voice, he continued. "I am going to need you to lie down in here." He proceeded to graciously direct me to his single bed in his bedroom.

I was excited about this turn of playtime events. Was I really getting to lie down during this game?

Guess what happened next?

He said, "And I may be awhile, so you can look at this magazine until I get back."

Lie down and look at a magazine? It had been years! "Doctor" had officially become my all-time favorite game.

As I laid down looking at a magazine, I was so grateful for my sons. I was so grateful for our relationship. I thought about how playing with my sons was exactly what I needed to do that day. It was so fun and refreshing. It magically gave me a clearer picture of my priorities for the day, which gracefully offered balance. "The Doctor" helped me realize that I had scheduled too much into my day. Balance is not only vital for our children, but it's also a requirement for parents. Balance is a secret ingredient for a happy home.

Then it was my turn to be the doctor, and I gladly put on the surgery scrubs over my clothes. After a bit more time, Isaiah decided that we were done at the doctor's office.

"Mom, could you take that off?" Going with his lead, I took off my current costume of surgery attire.

Then he very contently said, "Mom, I want to give you a hug." He didn't want to give his doctor a hug. He wanted to give his mother a hug.

We hugged as time slowed. I took in this sweet six year old presence. Then he ran off singing. Our playtime filled his soul with importance and love. It filled my soul, too, with perspective and the joy of motherhood.

I had chosen time with my boys over my busyness. It was powerful, indeed.

Hurry? Why?

Years ago, I had young Josiah in tow as I headed to Target. Hand in hand, we moved across the parking lot. Unsuccessfully, I tried to encourage his small legs and our pace to go a little faster.

"Hurry honey," I gently said to my precious little blond tike.

Innocently, yet oh so powerfully, he said, "Why Mommy? Why hurry?"

His words dramatically hung in the air. I slowed my pace because his quiet question hit me hard. I had no good reason. I had no real reason to hurry. I had no appointment right after our errand to Target. We had no place we HAD to be. I was just in the sad habit of hurry. With conviction in my heart that came from my small child with the small vocabulary, I humbly said, "Ok, honey! We don't have to hurry!"

One of my husband's favorite authors is Dallas Willard. In a conference we attended, Dr. Willard said he wants to live his life in such a way that he "Ruthlessly Eliminates Hurry." My son and this beloved author had the same heart on this crucial matter.

In addition, it was another one of the many mom moments that my children taught me a searching lesson that seeped into my soul. I don't have to move through my days with a cadence of busyness. We can choose our activities in such a way that we don't have to describe our days as "too busy."

I have learned much from our children over the years and I have also learned so much from my dear husband, George. During our first year of marriage, George helped me process this profound statement.

"We all are only given 24 hours in a day. We can't gain hours."

We must include sleeping in those 24 segments of time, so we may have 16-18 hours to prioritize the time God has given us each day. Parents often act helpless and complain about not having enough time; however, we all are given the same amount. No one is a victim of "not enough time."

Instead, we are all given the same gift and need to be responsible managers of those hours. I must choose wisely with those daily hours, so I don't have to hurry all day long! Habitual and constant hurry produces stress, pressure and anxiety in our children's heart, as well as ours.

When you see me at the grocery store, don't be surprised at my response when you ask me, "How are you?" I will not answer by saying, "busy." Will you be ready for me to say with a smile "Ruthlessly Eliminating Hurry?"

Even with our endless range of responsibilities, parents can very purposefully give their children the gift of balance. Our children motivate us to slow down, engage and live in the beautiful present.

A mom who is a flight attendant and gone a few days each month so articulately said, "Playing with my two kids makes me slow down and enjoy the moment. I never thought I would have to work on being present, but when I am, we are all rewarded."

Don't hurry through the day. Let's slow our cadence before we turn around and it's too late!

Jesus said, "Let the little children come to me and do not hinder them, for the Kingdom of GOD belongs to such as these." Mark 10:14

7

Preventer #5
Too Self-Conscious

Many parents struggle with play because it is uncomfortable. Maybe they didn't grow up with parents who engaged and played with them; therefore, it doesn't come naturally and playtime is simply out of their comfort zone.

My comfort zone is a game. With our two young sons at home, I would play a game with them any day. But, I would feel self-conscious and I would have an immediate pit in my stomach when our boys wanted to play "pretend."

I had the privilege of being the second daughter in a family of four girls. The toys that adorned our toy closets were Barbies and their horses, those adorable Fisher-Price people and their houses and school. My personal favorite was my mom's fancy dresses with sequins and frills. My sisters and I loved pretending. We would contently play for hours. I have many positive memories of playing with my sisters and my mom.

We grew up on a farm in Iowa. Our gorgeous six-acre property proudly displayed a beautiful barn, smoke house, two chicken coops and other antique-filled buildings. One of my most cherished memories was when my dad and mom remodeled a chicken coop into a playhouse. Out came chicken crates, old wood, cob webs, and a fair amount of junk. In came an old bed, an adorable retro small orange couch with matching chair and celebrated supplies for a pretend kitchen. My sisters and I were delighted! We adored that chicken coop and created many memories together playing, "Little House on the Prairie," "school," or "college dorm."

With some good old-fashioned blood and sweat from the entire family, the dirty chicken coop was transformed into a little retreat center with reused furniture, curtains and play dishes. Our pretend play was extensive and always included collecting items in a basket that I carried on my wrist. I always loved that basket and placing necessary items in it—unique leaves, rocks or my prized creepy crawlies. I am sure that the basket was inspired by Laura Ingalls.

Through the years in that playhouse, I was a teacher, student, a mother, daughter, college student, veterinarian, chef, a gymnast home after the Olympics, and a director of an orphanage. I developed quite an imagination, and I could pretend play with the best of them.

But when Isaiah was old enough to pretend play HE wanted to play cars. Unlike the make-believe world that my sisters and I enjoyed, my boys had other ideas. No, I had not been trained well for playing "cars." I was from a family of girls. How do you play cars anyway?

Furthermore, I was never a NASCAR driver in the chicken-coop-turned-playhouse. The former teacher in me wanted to make playing cars into a learning activity. I proposed that we sort the cars, count them, or let's line them up by size. We could even pick out our favorites.

That definitely was not satisfying to Isaiah. "No mom, let's play cars." "Play cars, what does that mean?" I had a brief sickening feeling that this was going to get ugly. Why? I simply could not make the right car noises. Even at his young age, my son's sound effects were simply amazing. I grabbed a bright red car and I sheepishly sat on the floor with my son. I quietly pushed the car on the rug and as energetically as I could I said, "Vroom Vroom!"

Isaiah hesitantly said, "Mom, cars don't say 'Vroom.'"

I decided I didn't like playing cars anyway. Didn't I have some laundry to put away? I don't like putting laundry away, but I liked playing cars even less.

However, my stronger motivation was a desire to connect with my son on that Monday morning. I had a motherly tenacity to keep trying. Isaiah had the same determination! He had a goal of teaching his mother how to make proper sound effects and within seconds, he had broken down the skill into minute steps. He was confident that this would be an effective lesson for his mother.

"Mom, put your tongue on the roof of your mouth!"

With hopeful anticipation I said, "Ok!" and, I obeyed.

"Now Mom, I want you to place your teeth together to the point that they are almost touching."

"Now I want you to say the T and D sounds together really fast."

"Ok, son, I will." We looked at each other with eyes of anticipation, and excitement! Sadly, the only thing that happened when I tried to follow Isaiah's sweet instructions was that he was doused with mama spit.

He tried. I tried. He knew I was embarrassed and self-conscious about my failed sound effects. Immediately, his goal changed from giving me success to giving me comfort.

"Mom, it is ok. You can make any car noise that you want." I settled into the reality that making realistic car noises was not one of my strengths. Perhaps, making sound effects was a male gene.

That night, I asked George how a boy so young could produce such amazing sounds from his little mouth. How does he know how to create the sound of shifting gears and slamming brakes? He agreed it may just be a male gene.

Although my sons always seemed to know just when to park their cars and had the perfect timing for a car accident, I did learn how to play cars. We would play traffic jam, parking lot and car races. However, it never came naturally and never was my favorite activity to engage in with my sons. Favorite or not, it sure did bring a lot of laughs over the years. Through the long and awkward moments of car-play, laughter often reigned. This leads me to the Power that accompanies parents and their self-consciousness in play.

Power # 5

Power of Laughter

Although playing with Hot-Wheels was never my choice when it was my turn to choose our activity, I sure did love the laughter that this activity would foster. Sometimes the laughter even came because of my failed sound effects. We would laugh and laugh, and it was a powerful part of any Monday morning or Thursday afternoon!

One mom with two girls agreed with me regarding the power of laughter. "It is hard to sit down and play, but I sure enjoy feeling close and laughing with them. It is so fun to giggle together."

Interestingly enough, this precious mother equated laughing with her daughters as feeling close with them. Just simply laughing with our children helps us to bond and feel connected!

On a Wednesday night in the summer, I walked the four kids to the park with a Frisbee in hand. We all picked a spot in the spacious end of the park. Quickly, we discovered how wet the grass was from the recent watering from the sprinkler. Playing Frisbee in the water-soaked lawn made us all laugh and laugh. We all craved the natural giggles. The boys all tried to get their feet as wet as possible. What did the girls do? Cartwheels of course! Silvanie and I decided to get our hands wet instead of our feet. The laughter of that wet Frisbee game was bonding and healing. I called George on his way home from work to meet us at the park to join in the laughter. His arrival at the park made it even more fun.

Humor and Health

Parents all over the globe have discovered the power of laughter, but so have the professionals. For over twenty years, research has conducted, the correlation between humor and health. Many studies confirmed the positive effects on the body and soul from laughter. Two researchers, Dr. Lee Berk and Dr. Stanley Tan of Loma University in California, studied the effects of laughter on the immune system. Their published studies have shown that "laughing lowers blood pressure, reduces stress hormones, increases muscle flexion, and boosts immune function by raising levels of infection-fighting T-cells, disease-fighting proteins called Gamma-interferon and B-cells, which produce disease-destroying antibodies. Laughter also triggers the release of endorphins, the body's natural painkillers."

We all know laughing is fun and good for us emotionally. But it is also good for us physically. The bottom line is that laughing produces a sense of well-being in us all.

Go Ahead! Laugh with Your Loved Ones!

What if we had a goal of laughing with our children each day? We would be so incredibly healthy! We love laughing with our co-workers or friends. We can also love laughing with our young ones, no matter what their ages. We can be intentional about connecting with a little humor in the hours we spend with our children.

Loving the Laughter

Recently, I had lunch at a new friend's home. She and her husband have one biological son and then adopted three children. Our bond was immediate and sincere. We had shared very few minutes together prior. But over sandwiches and green tea laced with fresh mint from her garden, we quickly found we have so much in common. Our conversation was off and running.

We laughed and lamented about the intensity of motherhood. We watched our seven children of various ages as they effortlessly went from jumping on the trampoline to playing in the large blown-up pool. Then the slip-and-slide came out, and I couldn't take it anymore. I had to join the fun. My kids had all brought their suits. But I just wouldn't let that stop me, even though I was afraid that I might hurt myself.

Maybe I shouldn't. I had just washed my hair this morning. I was also really enjoying my conversation with this dear new friend.

Even with all of the very obvious risks, I stood in line behind the seven smiling children. They were anticipating their next trick on the wet slide. Then it was my turn. I nervously ran and very hesitantly dove on the yellow plastic strip. This first attempt was a big bonk, but I wasn't about to stop now. Turn after turn, we laughed and laughed. Each time, I went a little farther and didn't appear too terribly old in my attempts.

At least the other participants were encouraging me to keep trying. We slid on our knees and stomachs and a few kids tried sliding across on their feet. I ended my slip-and-slide adventure with a cartwheel, of course.

The number of gut giggles that the simple activity fostered was so therapeutic for each laugher. It makes me laugh just thinking about it. We all went home so happy and thankful. I was thankful that I didn't let my pride or my sore back or my newly washed hair, get the best of me. I would have missed out on one of our summer highlights.

Humor and Highlights

A friend and teacher shared these valuable thoughts on play.

"I believe that play with our older kids is just as important as it was when they were younger, but perhaps for different reasons. When our children are small, play is an important and powerful vehicle for bonding and learning skills across all developmental domains. As our children get older, I have found that play can serve as a gateway to communication with a sometimes 'more difficult to communicate with' teenager. My teen responds much better to more serious topics of discussion (or any discussion, for that matter) after having just spent some time being silly and having fun laughing with me versus when I just slam her with it out of the blue! We spend time doing our hair and make-up in funny ways, we'll have a dance off, we'll change the lyrics to popular songs to make them goofy, or we'll make-up

**new rules or ways to play board games. After a good
laugh, it seems as if we are all more open and receptive to
communicating with each other about daily events, as well
as life's challenges.**

**Michelle Dalton from Oklahoma, teacher and mother of
three children: 14, 9 and 6.**

"Don't Leave, Mama"

"Don't leave, Mama. Stay. Just stay." Silvanie and I
ended a difficult day cuddling in her bed after story
time. We quietly faced each other as we lay on her
bed. We tenderly held each other's eyes and smiled.
I started making some funny faces, and she crinkled
her nose in the precious way that only she can do. I
love it when she does that! It is her sweet trademark.
We giggled and giggled. She eagerly waited for my
next created face. Then she giggled some more. The
frustrations of the day melted away into the long
moments of laughter. Our laughter bonded us together
at the close of another day. She fell asleep as I left the
room with a little laugh across her kissable lips.

Laughter! I love its power!

"Children will not remember you for the material things that you provided, but for the feeling that you cherished them."

~Richard L. Evans

8

Preventer #6
Too Task-Oriented

When asked, "Why is it hard to sit down and play with your child?" 70% of the parents' first response was, "I'm too task-oriented and my house calls me." Frequently, Moms and Dads feel like they can't play until all of their tasks are done and the house or yard is just right. They feel like engaging with their kids is a luxury that is only allowed after all of the work is done.

I don't know about you, but my work is never done and if I wait for that mysterious day, my kids would never have any focused attention from me.

If I wait for the pots, pans, paperwork, and planets to align before I can sit down with my kids, they would live their days "sorry out of luck" and longing for some eye contact from me.

After talking to a mother of three boys about the topic of play, she said with a heavy sigh, "I always feel like I have so many other things to do."

And my dear husband George said, "It is not that I don't want to play with our kids or that they are not a priority, but there is simply too much work that must get done in the few hours that I am at home at night. But I have learned the simple power of saying 'yes'. 'Yes, we can go on a bike ride.' 'Yes, we can kick around the soccer ball in the yard.' A 'yes' means we connected."

One Saturday, George and I were particularly task-oriented. At the time, we were a family of four. Instead of going hiking, we decided to stay home and take care of some tasks. My blood was beginning to boil with the anxiety about all that we wanted to get done. We started our tasks in the backyard. After some productive yardwork, I decided to play football with the boys. While we were casually tossing the ball to each other, one son said, "Mom, I forgot to tell you that I lost a LEGO piece out here in the grass. Could you help me find it?"

I wanted to say, "Find a LEGO in the grass? Are you kidding me?"

As a mom, I have developed a special definition of LEGOs.

LEGOs — colorful plastic pieces that provide hours and hours of cool creating, discovering

and inventing. These small important pieces provide entertaining play. Many pieces will get lost and then gloriously found, but this will take a lot of time and effort from the whole family.

Important fact: The smaller the piece, the more important it is. The more important the piece, the larger the frustration when lost. These creative bricks will foster a wide range of emotions for all involved. You can count on joy and excitement to be experienced by all LEGO Masters. Enjoy!

With a determination inspired by love and good deeds, I said, "Just a minute, honey. I will be right back." Out came a plastic magnifying glass so that we could play "detective." We crawled around and around in the brown grass, dried from the Colorado summer heat, carefully looking for the LEGO piece. We took turns with the official detective's tool and peered deep into the grass, so hopeful that we would uncover the lost LEGO piece.

At one point while we were on all fours, we bumped into each other. Isaiah said, "Mom, this is so much fun!" I really thought so too, but I was amazed by his response.

We didn't spend any money for this playtime to be "so much fun." We didn't leave the house and participate in a big event for this to be "so much fun." We didn't even get any toys out except an old magnifying glass for this activity to be "so much fun."

We were just spending time together and we didn't even find the LEGO piece.

If tasks, long lists and your "to-dos" are the focus day after day, then the Power of Relationship will help you to reprioritize so you can pause and play!

Power #6

Power of Relationship

It was 8:44 p.m., and the kids were finally heading to bed after a fun summer Friday night at home! While the two younger kids moved into the bedtime routine, George and Josiah ran to the grocery store to pick up a few needed items for an early morning Track Meet for the boys. Like always, I looked forward to my children's bedtime so I could tackle tasks that had been waiting for me all day.

Sweet Silvanie quietly came to my side and said, "Can you read me a story or no?" My heart sank! I had forgotten to read to the kids and then when I realized it, I had secretly thought I was actually getting away with not reading to them tonight! I stopped short. Silence filled the room with my indecisiveness.

Leaning in closer, she softly persisted. "Can you read me a story or no?"

Moments after I finished a peaceful cuddled up story time with Silvanie and Bernard, I sat down with my "list," to accomplish one task. Maybe even two! The second I sat down, the runners were back from the store and Josiah came to my side and joyfully said, "Let's finish our Monopoly game mom, ok?" I smiled and said, "Yes."

We proceeded to play our third night of National Parks Monopoly. Josiah seized the victory with Mom's bankruptcy. How do my boys always seem to acquire a "guaranteed win" with being the first to land on "Broadway"?

These innocent, endearing, but sometimes overwhelming requests from our children desiring us to play with them often greet us throughout the day!

Every day a war in every home rages: The battles of Tasks versus Relationships. During our days, are we more focused on our tasks or the beloved relationships in our home? Of course, from dawn until dusk there is a list of daily tasks we need to complete.

In our home, our common morning madness sounds like, "Mom, I need some socks." What is it about my battle with the socks? Washing, matching, finding them under the couch, bed or swing set. Having socks for everyone is one of a million tasks that demand my time. My friend's solution to her battle with socks is that they don't need to match. She calmly and victoriously shared that her boys never go to school with matching socks. It is not a priority to her or them, so she doesn't spend time matching them. I am going to think about that one.

Playing Parent or Preoccupied Parent?

Do we push our children aside day after day so we can tackle the tasks? At some point in the week, we have to ask ourselves, "Have I been a playing parent or a preoccupied parent?"

One day, I had a relentlessly hard day with one of my children. Whining and negative behavior reigned. Don't assume the whining and negative behavior came from the child . . . maybe it came from this mama. I had a desperate attitude in my heart that wanted this child far far away. Instead of pushing him far far away, I realized that I needed to pull him close. It had been a task-oriented few days, and we hadn't played. Playing with him absolutely changed his demeanor and behavior. As I sat there, I could literally observe his tank filling.

We reconnected. This reconnection promoted a better demeanor in both of us. He dropped his negative attitude and I dropped mine. The attitude, that just moments before wanted him far away changed to wanting him as close possible. As we played our simple game, I looked in his face, his bright eyes, and his contagious smile.

During its successful run for seven seasons on ABC, I saw a few episodes of the British Supernanny. In her reality show, Jo Frost, a professional nanny, was committed to partnering with parents and children so that all of the members could experience success, joy, and positive relationships in family life.

I agreed with her many mottos and her practical tips for discipline and family dynamics. I loved her "Positive Alternatives to Saying No", "How to Avoid Parent/Child Power Struggles" and her "Stay Calm Strategies."

If I could ever sit down for a cup of tea with Ms. Frost, I would praise her for her 100 episodes. Then, I would also ask her to add one more motto. My added motto would be:

"Have you played with your child today?"

Many times when our children's behavior is tiring to our nerves and trying our patience, we are left with the desperate question, "Where did this behavior come from?"

Do we really want to know? It might be more simple than we think and more profound than we want to admit.

Often, the behavior comes from the child's need to spend some focused time with mom or dad. They just need some calm and peaceful time with us.

When Josiah was 18 months, it seemed like literally overnight, my joyful JoJo turned into a behavior challenge. I vividly remember thinking, "If I am going to start disciplining him, I also need to intentionally start playing with him."

I remember fondly pursuing my little son in play after dropping off Isaiah at morning kindergarten. We played puzzles and play-dough and enjoyed peek-a-boo. Our playtimes were magical, and many defiant behaviors were curbed as quickly as they started.

If we don't have a relationship with our children, who are we to really think we can appropriately and lovingly discipline?

"Playing with my kids—really enjoying each other helps to diffuse tense situations later," a wise mom told me as we talked about play.

She knows, I know and you know that tense situations occur every day. The most effective way to diffuse tense situations and power struggles is if we have already connected with our kids in a positive manner by the time the tense situation comes our way. Then the negative or difficult moment or situation is not quite so heavy and draining.

Connecting with our children can curb our anger and can literally produce patience.

When I feel the distinct need to raise my voice or impose discipline, I try as hard as I can to keep eye contact with the recipient. It is amazing how all can remain calm and bright when I keep eye contact with that cutie pie.

If I yell across the house or while my head is face-down picking up toys, I can't make the needed connection, and all calm is lost.

Indeed, play promotes more effective discipline so that our relationship can remain the priority. Even in our correction, we can stay tuned into our connection. Play also develops intimacy in our relationship and it takes us to a place of discovery about our children.

After devoting time to her daughter, one mom said, "I didn't know my daughter knew her ABCs. When did she learn that?"

My son and I sat down one afternoon to play UNO and he said, "Mom, did you know that I am a gentleman? I am going to let you go first." I was so glad to learn that he was now a gentleman.

When we engage through eye contact, couch connection and a card game, we communicate to our children that they matter. However, when tasks win the war week after week, relationships are damaged and torn apart. Building intimacy with our children must be a priority.

We need to put down our tasks so we can truly connect. Let's literally push the pause button and play.

"All we have to decide is what to do with the time that is given us."
J. R. R. Tolkien

9

Preventer #7
Too Distracted

Let's be honest! The loud singing of just the chorus 100 times, the long reciting of math facts, whining, complaining and endless noises can send us into a place of e-x-h-a-u-s-t-i-o-n. Sometimes we need to regroup. Some days we deeply crave a distraction from it all.

George and I have the loudest children on the block. We may even have the loudest children on the planet. Most often, it is a joyful noise that echoes through our walls and out our opened windows. Some days, the noise is anything but joyous, and I search for a momentary distraction.

Unfortunately, our momentary distractions can steal more time than we realize or intend.

We love and live in an HD world. Instead of HD standing for High Definition, I would like to suggest that HD stands for Highly Distracted. In our trendy society, our distractions are often in the shape of a small rectangle.

Go anywhere and you will see men, women, moms and dads staring at these classy looking rectangles. These devices not only make and receive phone calls, but now we have our e-mails, Facebook, and other data available anytime, anywhere.

One company's recent commercial proudly boasted of their newest plan—unlimited talking, texting, and data. How great is that?

It just may be great for your growing business.

But when it comes to parenting, I am afraid, it is not so great. Of course, there are benefits to our advanced technology. I may even own a smart phone one day, but I personally don't need one more distraction.

One night, I was on a date with my eldest son, Isaiah. We faced each other in the booth very happily stuffing our faces with fresh guacamole and chips. We talked about God, girls, and the great food. As always, he made me laugh so hard that I cried, and we thoroughly enjoyed our hours together. Between laughs, I kept noticing the people in the booth right behind my son.

A son about Isaiah's age and his mother painfully ate their meal. How do I know they were mother and son? They looked exactly alike with their curly hair and similar facial features. The boy rested his head in his hand and seemed bored, annoyed, and miserable. He stared blankly into his unfinished hamburger and ketchup covered fries. His mother wasn't asking about his day, his highs and lows or his dreams. She wasn't asking him anything because she was on her phone . . . the whole time! The waiter finally gave them their check. They silently left the restaurant. The handsome son looked over at our table as he passed by.

I didn't have a critical heart towards the mother. I had a sad heart for them both!

Whatever she was dealing with could have waited. She may have been talking to her boss or talking to her best friend, but I don't really care. She could have told them that she had an important appointment and date with her son. She could return the call when her son wasn't sitting across the table, waiting for a little focused time from her.

In the blink of an eye, this young teenage son will be driving and a night with his distracted mother will be last on his list of priorities.

She was highly distracted! Our society is highly distracted. Sometimes I am highly distracted.

What distracts us and creates a barrier from eye contact and engaging?

Sometimes it is our cute gizmos and outward noises: like the computer, Facebook, T.V., smartphone , cell phones and our schedules.

Sometimes what distracts us is our inward noises: like worry about an upcoming event, frustration from rejection from a friend, fear from a hard season in marriage, or regret from a devastating decision.

The inward and outward noises are sometimes relentless. We are desperate for an escape from the noises, so we turn to our distractions and turn away from our children.

What are your current distractions? Go ahead — write them down.

_____

_____

_____

_____

_____

_____

I have a love/hate relationship with Facebook. I have only been a "friend" on Facebook since 2010. I finally gave into the pressure that I was receiving from none other than my precious mom. Since we live in different states, she wants to keep up with her grandchildren through frequent photos and anecdotes. Even as a 42-year-old woman, I still like to make my mom happy, so I made a reluctant and late arrival into the social networking world.

Facebook presents great opportunities. I love keeping in touch with friends and family. I love wishing cousins and aunts Happy Birthday. I love seeing your families, keeping in touch with long-lost friends from high school or someone I used to teach with, posting an encouraging Bible verse or recent photo.

However, I hate the time stealer that it is. I hate weeding through information that is really not Facebook worthy to see an important post that I was grateful that I saw. No offense, but I don't really need to know where you ate on Friday night, who you were with, or about your Starbucks drink that you retrieved on your way to work.

Because of the reoccurring noises in my home and heart, I find myself drifting to the screen of Facebook and escaping for "just a minute." Unfortunately, I have learned the strong pull of the FB opportunities and how important individual guidelines are. The "just a minute" steals more time than I ever desired or sometimes realized.

I am not the only one who needs media mentoring. Greek triple jumper Voula Papachristou found herself disqualified from the 2012 Olympics in London because she tweeted a racial comment to a friend. In earlier years, it was a positive doping test that would disqualify an athlete from displaying their excellence for the whole world to see, but not in this new media mania. Now it is negative tweeting. Get ready to pack up your team uniform and the short-lived glorious global greatness if the social media policy is not followed.

If the Olympic athletes need to go over social media etiquette, so should families. Each member in the family would benefit from the discussion of his/her personal involvement in this networking phenomenon.

I see nothing cool about seeing a group of friends out and about on a Saturday night with their faces and fingers completely enthralled with their time stealers. They have friends surrounding them. If they aren't going to enjoy and engage with the people they are with, they should have just stayed home in their jammies.

I also grieve when I see a pool filled with children laughing and swimming, while their mommies are on the side of the pool with their smart phone, not at all concerned with using the time to make a summer connection.

What are some appropriate guidelines for our highly distracted culture? Because I don't want anything to steal my time without asking, here are my three personal social media guidelines.

1. I try not to be on FB when my kids are around.
2. I stick to 15 minutes a day.

3. No FB on the Sundays. The important posts will have to wait until Monday. If your birthday was on Sunday, I do apologize for my late wish of happiness. If you see me post something on Sunday, you can message me to get off.

I don't want to succumb to our HD culture. I don't want the distractions to characterize my life. I want to be a focused wife, mother, daughter, sister and friend.

What technology guidelines would benefit you and your family?

Power # 7

Power of Focus

"Stay focused," I said to my four children as each was folding a pile of clean laundry. I had tried everything to help make the weekly folding be a successful team project. I had tried rewarding the kids with M&Ms, money, and meanness. Each had been equally unsuccessful.

On this Monday, I had each child fold a pile of clothes in a different location. No one could touch each other, knock down someone's folded pile, or argue about who had matched the most socks. As I left each area, I reminded each child to stay on task.

As I cooked dinner, the helpful four folded their piles from different corners of the house. As they folded, I heard joyful singing and talented rapping. Some piles were neater than others. A couple of the kids called me in to give a helping hand, but piles were folded. Hallelujah! Success! At least for this week's folding session. Then it is the "put away party."

Once again, I heard myself say, "Stay focused," as they crammed clothes into their drawers filled with wonderful used garments given by generous friends.

As a family, I want to be able to be focused when doing our "high fives" (our chores), homework, or pulling weeds in George's garden. There are so many distractions during these times, so "stay focused" is necessary verbiage.

But more importantly, I want to have a razor sharp focus on the hearts of my children. To maintain that focus, I must fight against our highly distracted culture.

The Heart of the Matter — Their Hearts

I want to be connected to my children's souls. Their hearts are really the heart of the matter. I don't play with my children so that I can be remembered as the world champion of Skip-Bo. I play with them because I want them to know they are dearly loved and cherished. I want them to know that I am available to hold their hands and to hold their hearts.

"Is Home for a Long Time?"

One night after some sweet one-on-one time with Bernard, we just sat on the couch and cuddled. His extremely high energy level always comes to a calming stop when we play together. While we snuggled, we just stared at each other and smiled. No distractions were allowed into this precious time. He quietly sat with a content and full heart. I gazed into his big, brown, gorgeous eyes. Like all children in the world, he soaked in this personal time. I did, too. It is always renewing.

Without warning, he said, "Is home for a long time?" Startled once again by his deep questions about his past, present, or future, I needed to let his question marinate. For 2 ½ years, his questions were always small pictures into who Bernard was and where he had been. **We** had a million unanswered questions about his past.

But **his** questions were special windows into his soul, and I was always so grateful for them.

I quietly replied, "Yes, Bernard. Home is for a really long time. Home is forever." I wanted to say more, but more was not needed.

"Are you glad about that, son?"

With a smile that would warm anyone's heart, he said, "Yes!" He wanted to say more, but more was not needed.

I thanked God that Bernard and I had some engaged time together. Our special time together communicated that I was available for him, and allowed him to ask a pressing question that was on his heart. I was humbled and grateful that I had made time for him.

I care about his heart. I care about the deep needs hidden in the hearts of all four of my children. We get to peer into their hearts when we have made room for them in our day.

Goals

Each season, I write down my goals. I write down spiritual, professional, and physical goals. I make home improvement goals and HOME improvement goals. The HOME improvement goals are the family goals. My goals are measurable and manageable.

I don't want week after week and month after month to pass by without focusing on our HOME improvement goals. George and I recently revised our family's mission statement. It helps us keep focused on what matters most to us. Do you have a mission as a family? What guides your family through your days and seasons of life?

Jakab Mission Statement

As a family, we desire to set our hearts on things above and not on earthly things. We want to clothe ourselves with compassion for those in need and kindness to those in our daily lives. We want to demonstrate humility and patience for each other. We want to forgive as God has forgiven us. We will pursue the Word of God, so He can dwell in us richly. Whatever we do, we want to do it all in the name of the Lord Jesus. And we will be thankful.

(Based on Colossians 3)

"It was character that got us out of bed, commitment that moved us into action, and discipline that enabled us to follow through." Zig Ziglar

10

Plan for Play

Like any other discipline, we just have to get started. However, whether starting a new running regiment or new organizational tactic, the first step is to have a vision and a plan. Next, filter your decisions through your visions and plans.

A Vision

Here are a few of our visions for our family:

A calm home life where connection, not conflict, reigns.

A space where all four children know they are precious in our eyes and God's eyes

A schedule that communicates to our children that they are a top priority through plenty of time to play!

A marriage that communicates love and respect, while giving our children a firm foundation.

A Plan

Below are my points for a plan to help you get started or keep you in the game of pursuing your children through play.

- ❖ Sometimes our fear is simply this, "After I enter the play world, how do I exit the play world?" "Am I going to have to play all day?" Many times when I play with my children, they are the ones who are ready to be done and they go off singing.

- ❖ Before my kids were school age, I always tried to play with my children right after we cleaned up from breakfast. This communicated that they were a priority in my day. Furthermore, I wasn't putting them off all day long. There is nothing like starting the day with a little connection with my kids.

- ❖ After I pick up the boys from school, I make myself available for the first 30 minutes after our arrival home. We talk on the couch or play a game, but I want them to know I am available for them.

- ❖ Some days are Work/Play Days. My kids now know this phrase and often ask, "Is this a Work/Play Day?" I sit and play a game for a 20-minute time period and then work for 20 minutes. Then I come back and we play, color or read together again. Then I go and work again. These days are almost magical. The kids are happy and content when we are together, but they are also happy and content to play by themselves because they know I will return soon. Furthermore, I stay on task because I know I have just 20 minutes to complete a job before I return to LEGO Land or Candy Land.

❖ Some days my kids choose the activity. Some days I choose. I usually choose something that doesn't have anything to do with sound effects.

❖ Are all moments in the world of play angelic with my children running off singing? Of course not. Some days the play ends in tears and timeouts; however, I always try to keep the bigger picture in mind — Positive Connection.

❖ If you are a list person, add "playtime" to your daily list. Victoriously cross it off when you are finished painting outside or coloring in their favorite animal coloring book on the floor.

❖ In the middle of your busy errand day, go to the park as one of your stops. And for the love of all children, keep your smartphone in your car. Your sweet little phone will be okay unattended. Your sweet little children may not be.

❖ Add props whenever possible. Props will keep both you and your children engaged and focused. For instance, retrieve Priority boxes from the Post Office. Use stickers for stamps and you are set. My kids loved writing addresses on the boxes and "mailing" a wonderful package to Grandma or Oma from our simple Post Office that we set up in the family room. My children learned to write their names and other words with this activity.

❖ Now that I have three children in school, my time with them obviously looks differently, but is still focused time and as crucial as ever. Friday Night game night, hikes or bike rides on Saturday, family devotions during the week, family walks and foot massages on Sunday are just a few of our faithful traditions.

❖ I try to grab built-in moments to connect. After I pick up Josiah from school, we have about 20 minutes to wait for Isaiah. I keep a Frisbee and a blanket and books in the car, and we are ready for action while we wait for Isaiah.

❖ Do I still play with my teenager? Indeed! Some days it looks a bit different from his early childhood, but some days it doesn't look different at all. He still loves a good game of Probe or Phase 10 and even enjoys playing "house" for a few minutes. He makes the best "Butler" with the salty snacks that he provides on a tray. It is quite enjoyable to play harder games as the kids get older, although I still can't get my mind around chess.

❖ There is sometimes a bit of tension in the children's hearts when we play a game because everyone wants to win. During game time, I repeat this helpful line a few times. "We play for three reasons. We play to learn, have fun, and be together." This motto came to my desperate mind early on in parenting when my kids would have such a fit when they didn't win. Sometimes I ask my kids to repeat the motto. It has benefited our family greatly for many years through wins and losses.

❖ Pack it in. Pack it out. When we go camping, I pack cards and games. When we go to the pool, I pack cards and a checkers game that is on a towel checker board. A 20-minute game does wonders and gives the kids a break from the sun or intense level of activity.

❖ No matter how hard the day has been, or how many tricks I exhausted during the afternoon, or how deep I had to dig to keep my patience intact, when we sit down to play, all that is set aside. My goal is to smile, look into their eyes, laugh, and make peace for our souls.

❖ Do I ever say "no" to their request for play? Of course I do.

❖ Am I ignoring my children the rest of the night after we have played? Of course not. We are folding laundry together, making dinner together, or they are playing their loud energetic games together.

❖ Some of you may be saying, "I don't know how. I don't know how to play." That is ok. Just go with their lead. They will teach you. If they ask you to play Super Heroes, you can simply say, "I don't know how, but you can teach me." They will be so thrilled to show you the ropes.

❖ One day, my boys wanted to play Super Heroes and I sure didn't know how to do that. I decided to watch for a minute. As I tried to get my bearings on the boys' current game of choice, I learned something very helpful. They were just playing tag with . . . sound effects. So I chose my super suit and super powers. My boys want a nice description of both. My suit was coral with tight black leggings. My super powers consisted of teleportation and the ability to freeze time. Every mom needs that super power. Then we played a glorified game of tag, with twirls and jumps. It makes a parent feel pretty super!

❖ On the day when you don't know what to play, just sit down on the floor or couch. It is amazing. In very short moments, you will be surrounded by your munchkins because they noticed you were sitting down. They will quickly see your contentment and attitude and will be filled with ideas of play. I often tell myself throughout the week, "just sit down, mom, and engage."

❖ If you despise crafts, that is okay. Find the area of play that you enjoy and run with it. If you are a game person, get some great age-appropriate family games. If you love to paint, pull out the smocks and paint away. When's the last time you painted a sunset for your child with washable paint?

❖ Except for a few things over the years, like Carr St. Café, our playtime has not been complicated. Don't make it harder than it needs to be.

❖ Some of you Type A personalities are saying, "Just give a time limit. How long do I have to do this?" I hesitate to give you a time because I am not the expert, nor do I want you looking at your watch. I want you looking in your child's eyes. However, I do have a desire to make these suggestions as practical as possible.

❖ The interviewed parents played with their children an average of 37 minutes a day. My personal goal is to play 30-60 minutes a day during the school year with each child or with all of the children as a group. The summer allows much more extended playtime with hours of play at a time.

❖ Sometimes a special location offers a wonderful opportunity for play, like the chicken coop/ play house when I was a child. Choose a creative place in your house or yard for your special engaged time with your child. The traditions and the memories will be rich.

Over the years, I have also collected ideas from other parents to guide us in our adventures with our kids of all ages.

❖ One mom, age 54, who parents a one-year-old and has a grown child, said she plays half an hour in the morning and half an hour in the evening.

❖ Another mom said that she plays for half an hour every day, and she incorporates a game night once a week. It is not a set night, but they make it happen sometime during the week.

❖ A mother who works during the day as a writer plays a game with her fifth grade son every day after school. This fun time starts their evening together. What a wonderful tone she sets, as the game time helps them both decompress.

❖ A mother of an infant enjoys strolling to the park and pushing her child on the swing for long periods of time. While swinging, they play peek-a-boo and sing.

❖ Another dad loves wrestling with his toddlers and makes that their daily connection.

❖ A mother of four kids ages 6 to 1 engages with her children through science and art each day, whether digging in the back yard or creating big posters with feathers and macaroni.

❖ A dear friend and mother of boys ages 22, 12 and 10 said, "We have to be willing to evolve with our kids and adapt to their interests over the years." Now that her boys are older, they often connect through sports, whether it is jumping on the trampoline or going for a run together. "They grow up so fast. It is up to us to mold them. Playing doesn't stop when they stop playing LEGOs." A few years ago when dirt biking became a newly loved activity for all of the boys in the household, this mom didn't just sit back at the campsite reading a book. Reading in a lawn chair would have been more comfortable for sure. Instead, they also bought mom a dirt bike and off they went during their camping trips. As a family, they would ride deep into the beautiful back country in the mountains. "We ride, we laugh, and we stop for a picnic that we packed." With many memories stored away in their soul, they connect on their dirt bikes.

❖ George connects with his four by letting the kids have an active role in the garden. They help choose the vegetables in the planting season.

They help water and weed. They victoriously bring in their produce during harvest time. Now they are at the age when they are starting to cook with the vegetables they grow.

❖ A mother of children ages 13, 10, and 6 enthusiastically said, "Playing with our children is how adults become their people. Playing is how we win them over." This mom tries to play with her kids every day. Their play may be a board game or soccer in the back yard. She also tries to initiate physical activities whenever possible. During her son's soccer practice, she will be found on the sidelines doing cartwheels with her daughter.

"It is not about just taking them somewhere. It is about being with them while you are there. My kids often say, 'Mom, did you see me? Did you see that?' Playing with them is how they know we see them."

When they know we see them, they know we love them.

❖ A dad of young ones frequently cuddles and reads to his kids, encouraging an activity to naturally flow from the story.

❖ A mom who works from home and has two school-age children schedules her playtime. "If it is important to me, it gets on my calendar."

Accountability to Our Own Reality

Wouldn't it be amazing if we held each other accountable for playing with our children as a routine topic of conversation? Instead of asking each other what reality show we watched this week, we could ask each other how is the reality of playing with your kids this week? How did you connect with your kids today?

"Children are too important and too intensely loved by God to be left behind or left to chance . . . Today they may snuggle into your lap, if you let them. But tomorrow you may not have access to them in the corridors of power they might occupy. Now is the time . . ."
Dr. Wess Stafford

11

Two Questions in the World of Play

After speaking on the topic to hundreds of moms, I am always amazed at the consistent response. Interestingly enough, two main questions are always asked. I will be addressing the first. Then my dear friend will address the second.

1. **How do you play with a large age span of children?**
2. **How do you implement play as a home school mom?**

1

Over the years, this first question is always asked either from a mom who stands in line to talk to me or from a mom who can't stand waiting to ask her question and she calls out from the audience and says, "I have five kids and they are newborn to 12. How do you handle that with regard to play?"

Sometimes I really want to say, "I don't really know. Just try it." I don't like the questions because by no means am I the expert. But since I have a wide range of kids myself, I am willing to share ideas and one word.

Intentionality

Choosing to be intentional to engage with our children is more realistic than we think. It takes discipline, but is so beautiful.

Intentionality can best be explained by telling you about a couple of nights at the Jakab home.

We play a board game for the older boys, while the two younger kids sit on our laps and "help." The next day, I play Memory with the younger kids, and the big kids gladly join in, as it brings back memories of their favorite game when they were younger.

The next night, we walk to the park and play soccer and everyone participates. (Silvanie doing constant cart wheels all around us during the soccer game is considered participating).

One day I draw pictures with construction paper with the three younger kids. I ask Isaiah to join us, and he stays at the table for a little while and then finishes his homework.

One day I read and read from Shel Silverstein's, *Where the Sidewalk Ends*. Everyone loves being together and listening.

One day Isaiah had a friend over and the two younger kids were fully engaged with each other. Josiah wandered around the house seemingly a little lost. "Mom, will you play with me?" On that day, he was the one who needed a little playmate.

Some nights after the two younger kids go to bed, we play a game like Scrabble.

Seize the Simple

There is no right or wrong way to play with a wide range of ages in your household. I strongly feel that being intentional and wearing playful eyes will prompt you in the right direction. Intentionality will guide you in the current need of connection. Sometimes we make it harder than it needs to be. My motto these days is "seize the simple."

If your kids are excited to have a water balloon fight in the backyard, put your worries aside for just a little bit and go get wet.

If your kids enjoy being outside, go outside with them and see what adventures you can enjoy.

There will always be something going on that will prevent you from playing with your kids unless you embrace the simple ways to play. We have a tendency to think and say:

"I will play with my kids when our move is over."

"I will make it a priority when the holidays are over."

"I can play with Tom, Dick, and Harry after we host the party."

"I will connect with them when school is out."

Now is the time. Be intentional to engage with your children, whether you have one child or eleven children. Choose to see the need in your children's eyes that they need some time with you.

Intentionally engaging—it is just a value choice.

2

The second question that I am often asked is from home school parents. "How do I add play to my home school day?" Since I have not home schooled, it is not my place to address this topic. I asked my dear friend, Amanda Hall, to tackle this important question.

Help for the Homeschooling Parent: Amanda Hall

I am privileged to address the home school parents. I know it is a challenge to think about playing with our children amidst our busy home school days. I'm a home schooling mom of three boys, ages 4-8 (with a little girl on the way). If your life is anything like mine, you hardly have time to go to the bathroom on school days. I want to encourage you that being a playing parent IS something you can do in the midst of your full-time job as teacher and that it will actually change your outlook on your day with your kids and help you to enjoy the role of "home schooling parent" a whole lot more.

One of the reasons I think we as home school parents have trouble finding time to play is because we need to take so much time each day to teach. The lessons must get done and ideally we'd like to get them done before dinnertime! I want to challenge you to think about how teaching and play can actually go hand in hand. As Cara discussed earlier in the book, play is a great way to teach! If you think about the times in your life when you have learned something well, there was probably some kind of "play" involved . . . whether it was manipulating objects or competing with someone in a game or some other activity that cemented the learning in your brain. If you see play as an avenue to learning and not a distraction from it, you will be more inclined to incorporate play into your day.

I also want to encourage you to think about why you chose to home school in the first place. Though there are many reasons people choose to home school, I think most would agree that having more time to develop strong relationships with our kids is near the top of the list. As Cara has shown, play is a fabulous way to develop those relationships, helping our kids to trust us more and enabling us to have more of an impact on their lives.

While I have a Master's Degree in Early Childhood Education and eight years of classroom experience under my belt, I am certainly not an expert in the area of play and I struggle with it all the time. The preventers Cara outlines in the previous chapters sure can get in the way. But I have found a few things that have helped me along the way, and I'd like to share those with you. (Thank you to my home schooling friends who have given me these tips over the years).

1. *Use play as often as possible in your teaching.* Ask yourself, "Can I teach or reinforce this concept with a game or some other playful activity?" It's ok to skip a page in the workbook if you find another way to teach the concept that will be more engaging and fun.

2. *Schedule playtime with little ones.* Don't just assume you'll find time for your toddlers and preschoolers in your day. They are easy

to shove aside in favor of the older ones' educational needs. Plan a block of time each day (preferably first thing in the morning) when they have your undivided attention devoted to playtime. Give your older children some independent work and instruct them not to interrupt while you spend this precious time with your little ones.

3. *Have a playful attitude.* Oftentimes, I get grouchy when there's a lot to get done and seemingly not enough time. Can you relate? Make it your goal to have a positive and playful attitude with your kids . . . smiling, laughing, and being silly whenever possible.

4. *Look for ways to play at uncommon times.* Turn on some music and dance around the kitchen with your kids when you are making dinner. Engage your kids in an age-appropriate game while driving in the car. Play a cleanup game at the end of the day with prizes.

5. *Enlist your children to help out with daily chores* so everyone has more time to play. We use "Accountable Kids," but any kind of structured system of responsibility and accountability for work done around the house will be a great benefit to your whole family.

6. *Draw your children into playful activities that you enjoy.* Recently, I found a word game on my Kindle that I like. I asked my twin 8-year-old

boys to help me with it, and we engaged in play together for a good long time.

7. *Accept the value of play.* As Cara shared, research shows that playing with young children contributes to future academic success. You can actually get a head start on home schooling by intentionally playing with your children when they are young.

8. *Take care of yourself!* This may not seem like it's related to being a good playing parent, but I assure you, it is! If you take the time to make sure your needs are met (eating, getting enough sleep, spending time with your husband or whatever needs you have), you will be better equipped to have a good attitude and right heart toward your children . . . and more energy to give them what they need.

9. *Take off your teacher hat at the end of the school day* and put on your playful hat for a little while. Take your focus off of assigning tasks and just enjoy time with your kids, like playing a board game or tossing the ball around, as a transition into the often crazy evening hours of dinner and bedtime.

10. *Focus your heart on Jesus each day,* who can enable you to have a happy and playful spirit. Ask *Him* to give you opportunities during the day when you can be playful with each of your kids and ask Him for the desire to do it.

"As the family goes, so goes the nation and so goes the whole world in which we live." John Paul the Second

12

Just Play

When you need to take a break from the stressors of the day—

Play with your children!

When you need to feel connected with your children—

Play with them.

When you need to relax and forget about your worries for just a little bit—

Play with your children.

When you need to talk to one of your children—

Play with them.

When you need to catch your breath from a week that literally has made you dizzy—

Play with your children.

When you want off of the train called, "life" and
want time to freeze—

Play with your children.

When your children are growing up too fast—
Play with them!

"Gotta Go Play with My kids!"

With tears streaming down her beautiful face, a classy
mom with long curly red hair walked up to me after
my presentation on this topic. I had just spoken to a
MOPS group meeting in the mountains. As previously
shared, this particular topic always seems to resonate
with moms and this morning was no different. With
sadness in her voice, her tears and emotions came
deep from her soul. "It never has even crossed my
mind before I heard you speak on this topic. My
house always looks great. My kids always look great.
But playing with my kids? It never even crossed my
mind. I take great care of my children, but I never
play with them." We talked for several minutes, and I
encouraged her by reminding her of all the ways that
she loved her children well.

I never want someone to leave a MOPS group feeling
guilty or shame. But I do have a strong passion to
encourage parents to be aware of our daily priorities
as moms and dads. Without awareness, we will have

countless missed opportunities to connect with our children.

I gave this mom a sincere hug. "You are a great mom," I said. I meant it. I could tell. With much sincerity, she thanked me. She looked straight into my eyes and said, "Thank you! Thank you so much! I gotta go. I got to go home and play with my kids."

"Me too," I said.

A Son and His Little Boat

Soon after that encounter, another mother waited to talk to me after I spoke at her MOPS group. She came up to me with a warm smile, introduced herself and said, "Thank you for sharing today. I am a Play Therapist". Oh boy, I was sure glad that I hadn't known that before I spoke. I would have been extremely self-conscious if I had known a professional "player" was in the audience.

She said, "Everything you said is right on. I play with children all day at work. I test them, I train them, and I teach them through play and I love it. But I struggle to play with my own children when I go home." She lamented how hard it is to stop and play. It was refreshing to have a heart to heart with her as we talked about this real issue.

She gracefully continued and told a story about her husband.

My husband grew up next to a little lake. He fondly remembers saving his allowance for a long time so he could buy a little boat. Finally, he had saved enough and he victoriously bought that boat. He couldn't wait to share the joy with his mother. "Mom, come out to the lake with me and I will give you a ride in my boat."

"No honey, I have too much to do today. Maybe another time."

"Mom, today I want to take you out in my boat. Please won't you come?"

"No honey. I am so busy. I just can 't."

With a strong determination, he asked again and again. Day after day. But, his mother always felt that she had more important and urgent things to do.

My husband tells the story with tears in his eyes and he says, "I remember the day that I asked for the last time. I stopped asking because I knew the answer would be "no". I was eleven years old."

The equally sad part of the story is that my sweet mother-in-law tells the same story about the boat. With tears streaming down her face, she shares that she always said "no" and she remembers the day that he asked for the last time. "He was eleven years old."

Both of us were moved by her husband's story. We encouraged each other to keep playing while our kids may be found. I am sure that this mother-in-law was a wonderful mom. There are so many tangible ways to demonstrate our strong love for our children.

But entering their world of engaging or playing has endless opportunities and benefits for us and our children that just can not be accomplished any other way.

Psalm 8:2 "From the lips of children and infants, God has ordained praise."

"Kids matter to God, so kids matter to us."
Awana International

13

100 Ideas of Play

1. Hide and Seek

2. Hide and Seek in the dark with flashlights.

3. Hide and Seek hiding a stuffed animal.

4. Hide and Seek hiding a glow stick.

5. Card games like UNO.

6. Skip-Bo

7. Blink

Any board games like:

8. Scrabble

9. Operation Shrek

10. Monopoly

11. Trouble

12. Parcheesi

13. Cadoo

14. Thomas the Train goes to the zoo (with plastic animals and labels for the animals that the child wrote)

15. Thomas the Train saves the day (role play that there is a fire using orange tissue paper and Thomas saves the people)

16. LEGOs

17. Doctor with clipboard, paper, money and insurance card

18. Restaurant with aprons and menu that child made

19. Post Office (get Priority boxes free from the P.O. Have stickers for stamps, money, address labels, and plain labels available. It is so fun to have your child write different addresses on the labels. It is a great and meaningful writing experience).

20. Grocery Store

21. Drive Thru

22. Role playing with Rescue Heroes

23. Scavenger Hunt

24. Ladder Ball

25. Relay races

26. Treasure Hunt with a map of the house that your child created.

27. Ship wreck — role play on your bed that you are in a boat

28. Draw together.

29. Create a book together like "Our Great Summer Days." Many printing stores can bind a book for you.

30. Read on a blanket outside.

31. Spin Art or painting with marbles

32. Play with Match Box cars or Little People on a cookie sheet filled with flour.

33. Play with Match Box cars or Little People on a cookie sheet filled with rice.

34. Measure and pour dried beans.

35. Measure and pour water in a big bowl at the kitchen table.

36. Magnetic letters on a cookie sheet

37. Charades based on a theme

38. Visit the park and you can slide down the curly slide too.

39. Cars with your talented sound effects

40. Barbies

41. Horses

42. Make an Amazing Race for your children. You take a turn too.

43. Football in the backyard

44. Soccer

45. Frisbee

46. Running together

47. Going for a walk

48. Bike rides

49. Hiking

50. Camping — our personal favorite

51. Nature walks

52. Play at the stream and throw rocks—show them how to skip rocks.

53. Lay in the grass after dark and star gaze.

54. Play in the rain.

55. Jump in the leaves together.

56. Build snowmen together.

57. Sardines—a game that is opposite of Hide and Seek. One person hides and everyone else seeks. When you find him/her, you quietly join them in their hiding place. You sit and wait until all of the teams or individuals found the group of hiders.

58. Tag and all of its variations

59. Show and Tell. We sit down together and everyone can show and then tell something about their day or week.

60. Super Heroes (just tag with sound effects)

61. Volleyball with a net or no net

62. Simon Says

63. Mother May I?

64. Red Light, Green Light

65. Climb a tree.

66. Jump rope.

67. Cut out pictures from magazines.

68. Paint at the table.

69. Paint outside.

70. Sidewalk chalk

71. Bubbles and balloons

72. Chess and checkers

73. Twister

74. Dance Party

75. Dance Party in the dark with flashlights

76. Play "city bus" by lining up chairs and making tickets.

77. Play house.

78. Play school.

79. Play church.

80. Make up games with empty egg cartons.

81. Make up games with empty milk jugs.

82. Collect rocks and paint them.

83. Gather leaves and make a picture.

84. Gather dandelions and make a picture.

85. Play family baseball.

86. Play dodge ball with wet sponges.

87. I don't usually like computer games for your time of connection, but one I do recommend is Hero Machine. Your kids can make a super suit for you too.

88. Draw family portraits.

89. Make strong holiday traditions.

90. Cook together. The kids are constantly helping me in the kitchen. We read the recipes together, measure and pour. This is a wonderfully engaged time. In the summer, we go a little deeper and I continue the tradition that my mom started with her four daughters. I have each child plan the meals and cook for a week. The kitchen provides a whole world of play. When Silvanie cooked this summer, she insisted on lots of tortillas. When it was Bernard's turn, you could expect a lot of meat scheduled in the menu. When Josiah and Isaiah cooked, breakfast food showed up all day long, like "Egg in the Basket."

My favorite part of the kid cooking is that when a child asks the daily question, "What's for dinner?" I can joyfully say, "You'll need to ask your brother or sister." We've made such sweet memories during our purposeful play over the stove and sink.

91. Read a chapter book together.

92. Keep a science journal as a family.

93. Keep a prayer journal as a family.

94. Sponsor a child and send them your letters and homemade pictures — more information about child sponsorship in the Recommended Ministries.

95. Serve a meal at a Rescue Mission.

96. Visit a nursing home whether you know someone there or not. Sing for them or take pictures that you made.

97. Make bread together and give a loaf to all the neighbors.

98. Do a family activity with Biblical truths. More information in the Recommended Ministries in the back of the book.

99. Read the Bible together.

100. Pray together.

With these 100 ideas, the goal is for you to engage with your kids with the activity. Too many times we have the mentality of occupying our children with something so that we can occupy ourselves with our agendas:

We allow them to be focused on technology for hours so that our children are not heard, and we can stay focused on what we need to get done.

We set up a play date so a child can play with our child, so we can finish a project.

We take them to the pool and we read at the side.

We take them to the park and then we talk to a friend on the phone.

We enroll them in many activities, so that we can focus on our ridiculously long to-do list.

At some point in our day, we need to stop looking down at our important work and start looking up into our more important work: our children's waiting faces and longing hearts.

Jesus said, "Those who drink the water
I give them will never again be thirsty."
John 4:14

14

The Power of our Living Water

I have always loved Father's Day. I have an amazing father and always loved the excuse to love on him a little bit more than usual. Of course, when I was growing up there were homemade cards, posters, and skits. Whether with a back massage or going out to eat, we loved honoring the man who was a perfect father for four girls.

My father was the man I loved holding hands with and talking to after school about any topic. No topic was off limits! I also loved working with him outside painting a fence together or creating a space for our new adorable baby ducks that he proudly brought home one day to surprise his girls. He always engaged with his daughters and made us a priority in his week!

I still love Father's Day and now I love honoring my husband as the father of our four children. He is strong, engaging, and committed. What a privilege to have a day set aside to honor these courageous men.

This Father's Day, we were on our annual Father's Day hike. It was a hot 100-degree sunny day and since we were hiking after church, we ended up hiking in the hottest part of the day. One of our favorite local hikes is Mount Sanitas in Boulder. At 2:00 p.m., we happily ventured out on our afternoon excursion. The heat enveloped us even as we started on the trail head. With determination in our steps, we began our 3,000 feet of elevation gain. Many weekends our family's "playtime" is in the form of a hike. We talk, laugh, and hold hands. We connect. For awhile I talk to George, then Isaiah, and then Silvanie wants a helping hand so she and I slow our pace. All the while, Bernard and Josiah jockey back and forth to see who can stay in the lead. We are always so grateful for these family hikes. The hikes, whether long, short, near or far, always reconnect us no matter how full the week has been.

On this Sunday afternoon, I repeatedly said "Happy Father's Day" to the men who were with their children. It was pretty obvious who was a family unit. With Silvanie by my side, we slowly hiked up the very steep incline. In front, I watched my precious man, hiking and talking to his three sons.

All the boys slowed their pace, so we could catch up with them and we continued. "Happy Father's Day," I said to a father who descended next to us as we were ascending. He looked at me with a surprised, but a pleasant smile. "Well, thanks!" he said. His daughter had the more surprised look without a smile upon her face.

"Today is Father's Day, Dad?" My heart sank for this father, who apparently was not going to be honored. George was sad for this man too and quickly said to the older teen daughter, "You better go home and make him a nice cake!"

Step by step we moved up the trail. The rocky and steep trail kept us alert. Our hearts were full, but George and I were concerned because there was one thing that wasn't full anymore and that was our water bottles. We had underestimated the amount of fluids we were going to need on this hot day. We had only brought three quarts of water, which was quickly becoming scarce. We became stingy with the kids' water intake and when they asked for some water, we encouraged them to keep hiking and we'd have water when we reached the top.

About an hour and half later, we joyfully accomplished our summit. We all gave each other high fives and we enjoyed big gulps of water. At the top, we talked to the people that had already summited, and I took a picture of George and the kids before we started down the mountain. This truly was family playtime at its best!

George and I looked at each other with smiles and love in our eyes for each other. However, we also looked at each other with a concern. We were now down to ¾ of a quart of water for the entire descent. That is not enough water for one person on such a hot day, and we had six thirsty people. Our resources were running low, too low.

On the hike down, we tried to think of ways to distract the kids from their tired bodies and dry mouths. I also quietly reminded them that there are people all over the world that have to walk this far just to collect water for their day's use. The preciousness of water is not an unfamiliar conversation in our household, but on this day the kids were not in the mood. I was ok with that; we kept hiking down.

Like it or not, the need for water was the main thing on our minds. One child kept repeating, "I am so thirsty, so thirsty."

One child was brought to tears and in desperation said, "Mom, I can't take it. I can't take it anymore. I am SO thirsty." Because of his asthma, I gave him another drink. We were down to the last sips. I caught George's attention, and he shared that everyone could have their last sip.

"Not too much. Don't drink too much, everyone needs one last drink." I wanted to sacrifice my sip for someone else. George lovingly insisted that I take a drink, too. Everyone gratefully drank one last sip before the gray sticker-covered Nalgene was empty.

Silvanie said, "Let me see. Let me see if there is anymore." She wanted to make certain that the water was gone. She peered intently into the bottom. The Nalgene was completely E-M-P-T-Y. After our last sip, we quickened our steps even more and continued.

Towards the end of the hike on the Sanitas trail, we noticed a gorgeous and unusually clear stream. When we arrived at the stream, the kids asked if they could drink. "No, it is not appropriate for drinking." It appeared so appropriate, but we refrained.

We had such a celebration when we arrived back at our mini-van, where quarts of hydration awaited. We didn't even care that the water bottles had not been in a cooler. We drank and drank and fell on the green grass in complete gratefulness for water!

W-A-T-E-R!

Oh! Water!

As I drank, I let it fall on my face. I pictured the water refreshing every ounce of my dehydrated body. The water was refreshing. I quickly thought of Jesus—my Living Water and my daily need for HIM to refresh my spiritual dehydration.

Holy Hydration

During Jesus' life-giving and life-transforming ministry on earth, He described Himself as the Living Water. This description was practical and personal. The description still changes lives today.

We can learn about this hydrating description in the book of John, chapter 4. Jesus is talking to a woman from Samaria. At that time, Jews did not associate with Samaritans. Furthermore, women at that time were second class citizens. Jesus was breaking two understood rules by engaging in conversation with her. The location of their conversation was the local well. Jesus was traveling to Galilee and had traveled through Samaria as his route of choice. He was thirsty from his walking travels and asked the woman, "Will you give me a drink?"

The woman, of course, knew the social norms and said, "You are a Jew and I am a Samaritan woman." It was if she was saying, "I am a Samaritan AND a woman. Two strikes against this conversation." She continues to question Jesus. "How can *you* ask *me* for a drink?"

Now her interest was piqued and she was ready to continue with this interesting man, who was unconcerned about the current rules.

Jesus answered her, "If you knew the gift of God and who it is that asks you for a drink, you would have asked him and he would have given *you* living water".

Of course, the woman questioned him about the meaning of living water. Was Jesus telling her that he had a higher status than their forefather, Jacob? (I have always liked that in the Bible times, last names were not even needed). She reminded him that he didn't even have a cup to draw water with and that the well was deep.

She was now fully engaged in this conversation.

Jesus answered, "Everyone who drinks this water will be thirsty again, but whoever drinks the water I give him will never thirst. Indeed, the water I give him will become in him a spring of water welling up to eternal life."

Never thirst.

Living water.

Water that is alive.

Sounds refreshing. I am sure that the woman at the well thought so too.

Jesus was not referring to physical water and drinking from the well at the center of town, or drinking water from a Nalgene on a hike, or from your kitchen faucet. Jesus was referring to a spiritual need that this woman had and that we all have.

We all have a longing deep in our hearts that only Jesus satisfies. We thirst. Sometimes the thirst is all that we can think about. We are distracted by our thirst. We often search and search for people, events, or things to satisfy our thirst. We find ourselves chasing after satisfaction. Sadly, we can be ruled and ruined by unsatisfied desires.

Only Jesus satisfies our thirst. He deeply satisfies our souls.

Scripture teaches that this woman had been married five times and that the man she was currently with was not her husband. Jesus knew she was desperately looking for a man to satisfy her. She had to keep searching for just the right man. She was looking for soul satisfaction. Jesus was saying, "Stop your search. I satisfy your heart and soul. No one or nothing else can." The work of Jesus always begins and ends in the heart. When we allow Him to heal and fill our hearts, we are satisfied. Completely.

This intriguing story in the Bible ends with a few more life-giving statements. The woman says, "I know the Messiah called Christ is coming. When He comes, he will explain everything to us."

With declaration Jesus said, "I who speak to you am He."

I love this story. The One and only Messiah that she had been looking for had come. He had even come and had taken the time to engage with her in her city. A gracious and life-changing encounter indeed. She would never be the same person. This simple daily water spot would never be the same place. For this is where she had met Jesus — her living water.

Adventuring without the Resources

On our Father's Day hike, we didn't take enough water. We are avid hikers; we should have known better.

But we happily set out on our adventure without the proper resource.

I didn't write this book because I have it all figured out as a mom. I did not write this book because I fabulously function with four children throughout my days. I didn't write this book because I am the perfect playing parent.

I did write this book because there are troubled children all around. Our children need us. They need our eyes, our smiles, our time and our hearts.

Let's not have even one more of our children grow up questioning if he was ever cared for, cheered for, or cherished. We can communicate that we care and cherish them by setting aside our Preventers and experiencing the Power of purposefully parenting.

In this very challenging culture, our children need a firm foundation. Firm foundations don't happen by accident. Firm foundations happen when we value our children and our daily reality is truly consistent with that value.

I did write this book because sometimes as avid parents we happily set out on our steep and rocky parenting adventure low on resources. I desire for this book to be a resource on your excursion of fatherhood or motherhood.

Lastly, I did write this book to share that during our adventure of parenting we need our most important power, resource and refreshment—our Living Water, Jesus.

I have a passion to engage with my husband and children. I love them each so dearly and deeply. Why wouldn't I make them a true priority? Most importantly, I have a passion to engage with Jesus.

Jesus is my most treasured gift and resource. Because of my daily-ness with him through Bible reading, journaling and praying, I experience him in personal and powerful ways. He ministers to me morning after morning. When I experience Him as my Living Water, my heart is full. I don't have to thirst for other people or things to fill me because my heart is already full and my cup overflows with his presence, peace, grace and goodness.

On a personal level, Jesus gives me the seven Powers

Rest—Psalm 91:1 "He who dwells in the shelter of the Most High will find rest in the shadow of the Almighty."

Memories—I reread my prayer journals each December/January and I am always in awe of God, His teachings and the rich memories of His sweet presence that gives energy and life.

Learning—Proverbs 2:1-5 "My son, accept my words and store up my commands within you, turning your ear to wisdom and applying your heart to understanding, and if you call out for insight and cry aloud for understanding, and if you look for it as for hidden treasure, then you will understand the fear of the Lord and find the knowledge of God."

Laughter — If you don't think that God has a grand sense of humor, you don't need to look further than a day in the life of the Jakab family.

Balance – I am reliant on Jesus to help me say "no" to the good, so I can say "yes" to the great.

Relationship—I have a personal relationship with Jesus. He is personally involved in my life, and I am desperately reliant on Him. Psalm 18:1 "I love you, O Lord, my strength. The Lord is my rock, my fortress and my deliverer."

If you have lived your life trying to sit on the throne, maybe it is time to surrender and to let the KING of all Kings sit on the throne of your heart. He has pursued you and desires to be a part of your life. He didn't just place the sun and stars in the sky, create the lions, leopards, and then create humankind just to then let them fend for themselves. He created you to have a relationship with you. He loves you so much that He died for you many years ago. Then He victoriously conquered death and rose from the dead.

We are all sinners in need of a Savior. You may be a good person. But you are not good enough. Your goodness is not the way to God. Jesus is the only way to God. Tell Him right now that you believe He is who said He was — the Savior of the World. He didn't just come to save the world. He came to save YOU. His forgiveness is a gift that needs to be received. Tell Him that you know that you have wronged others and wronged Him, that you need His forgiveness, and that you are done living your life on your own. Even as you read this book, He is there. Right there — ready to be the Lord of your life. Call on Him today. He's been waiting for you!

Focus — Colossians 1:9-14 "We have not stopped praying for you and asking God to fill you with the knowledge of his will through all spiritual wisdom and understanding. And we pray this in order that you may live a life worthy of the Lord and may please him in every way: bearing fruit in every good work, growing in knowledge of God, being strengthened with all power according to his glorious might so that you may have great endurance and patience, and joyfully giving thanks to the Father, who has qualified you to share in the inheritance of the saints in the kingdom of light. For he has rescued us from the dominion of darkness and brought us into the kingdom of the Son he loves, in whom we have redemption, the forgiveness of sins."

Because of Jesus, my preventers become powers and I am able to parent on purpose and with purpose.

Our Preventers Can Become Powers

Play is powerful, and it establishes a rich bond with our children. Play promotes rest, memories, learning, laughter, balance, relationship, and focus. Playing communicates that we have time for our children and establishes an open and loving relationship that will last a lifetime.

The Competition for Our Time Can Be Won for Today When We Engage With Our Child in Play.

Get ready for your stresses to quiet down and time to gloriously slow down during your engaged activity.

Playing with our children is just like any other discipline. We just have to get started; don't say, "I'm too tired, it's too messy, it's too boring, I'm too self-conscious, too busy, too task oriented, or too distracted." Instead, get a big glass of water, do a few stretches, put your game face on or in some cases put your pretend face on and play.

It is powerful!

Rock climbing in Moab
in 2008

New Year's Day tradition of
snowshoeing in 2009

Our first picture as a family of 6 taken
at God's Littlest Angels in Haiti

Our tradition of hiking
family fourteeners -
Mt. Huron, summer of 2009

In Iowa on my parents farm in 2010

Rock climbing as a family in
Keystone, CO in August 2010

Swinging with my kids on
the farm in Iowa - 2010

We have built many snowmen over the
years - family teamwork

Halloween 2012 - The boys and I will always
protect our princess, Silvanie.

New Year's Day tradition of snowshoeing
in Estes continues.

The love between the four was amazing from
day one, and we pray it always will be.

Family 14er - summer of 2012 - Mt. Democrat

We laugh together - we cry together - we play together

Epilogue

This summer, I saw a friend at the pool and we started talking about our kids. She said, "I saw you last week in the pool with your kids. I saw you playing 'Monkey in the Middle.' It made me laugh and it made me think that I should get off the side of the pool and stop watching my son. Instead, I should get in the pool and play with him."

We had a great discussion about the power of play. I asked her if she liked playing with her kids.

"Are you kidding me? I love it. It is just so hard to do it!"

Of course, I asked her the next question of "why."

She proceeded to say such a profound statement on this topic. "I feel like I am with my kids all day. Why would I need to play with them?" She continued with her depth. "But when I do sit down to play with them,

I am happy and filled. When I am with them all day, I have this longing to have some time to myself, but when I finally sit down to spend time with them, that longing disappears. I am no longer depleted and I am recharged."

A Season for Play

There will be a season that my house is cleaner. A season where my home-based business grows stronger, a season when I will finally get those new drapes ordered for the dining room and maybe even a season when I'll catch up on my scrapbooks. For this season, I am happy to play Monopoly or Headbanz. I'm content to create beautiful works of art with my children and proudly display them on the pantry door.

I am going to stop writing now. For Pete's sake, I need to go and play with my kids. You can stop reading now. For the love of your kids, you can go and play!

Sounds like my kids are laying down the tiles for a game of Rummikub, currently our favorite game. Maybe I will even let them win. "Wait for me guys! I want to play. Here I come."

As we gather around the dining room table together, we connect. We are not worried about the time of day, the floor that desperately needs a good mopping, the hand smeared windows or the unanswered e-mails.

We look into each others' eyes. Love abounds while time stops.

We are all present!

We all play.

It almost feels like Christmas morning!

About the Author

Cara Jakab treasured growing up on a farm in West Burlington, Iowa. She was one of four girls and loved being a part of her family's music ministry. They recorded three albums at the Bill Gaither Studio.

Cara is a wife to her best friend. Before they had children, she taught in the classroom for six years. She is a mother to her four gifts from God: Isaiah, Josiah, Bernard and Silvanie

Most importantly, she is a daughter of the KING.

She has a desire to daily put on the garment of praise and a passion to have her story bring God glory.

She believes each child everywhere matters to God, so she wants to spend her life advocating for children, near and far. You will also find her climbing up a mountain of laundry or climbing up a mountain in the Rockies.

She is available to speak on many topics. If you have questions about pursuing a life-giving relationship with Jesus or pursuing your children through play, she would love for you to visit her at:

www.aplayingparent.com

carajakab@aplayingparent.com

Notes

Chapter 3

    1. Forest Witcraft, One Hundred Years from Now. Excerpt from *Within My Power*. Scouting Magazine, 1950.

Chapter 4

    1. Webster's Dictionary
    2. Purvis, Dr. Karyn. Ph.D, Cross, David. Ph.D, Sunshine, Wendy. *The Connected Child*, McGraw Hill, 2007.

Chapter 5

    1. Kimmel, Dr. Tim. *Little House on the Freeway*. Sisters, Oregon: Multnomah Publishers, 1987.

Chapter 6

    1. Kimmel, Dr. Tim. *Little House on the Freeway*, Sisters, Oregon: Multnomah Publishers, 1987.
    2. Purvis, Dr. Karyn. Ph.D, Cross, David. Ph.D, Sunshine, Wendy. *The Connected Child*, McGraw Hill, 2007.
    3. Doe, Mimi. *Busy But Balanced*, New York: St. Martin's Griffin, 2001.

Recommended Reading:

Too Small to Ignore by Dr. Wess Stafford

Grace Based Parenting by Dr. Tim Kimmel

Little House on the Freeway by Dr. Tim Kimmel

When Faith Takes Flight by Jim Walters

Mothering Like the Father by Dianne Daniels

The Artist's Daughter by Alexandra Kuykendall

Recommended Ministries and Organizations for your family:

God's Littlest Angels is the orphanage that Bernard and Silvanie lived in for ten months. This life-giving ministry has many opportunities for involvement. Visit them at God's Littlest Angels online. You and your children can get involved and be a part providing hope in Haiti.

Compassion International is an amazing organization that is releasing children from poverty all over the world. Your family can get involved in deeply touching lives through monthly sponsorship and writing letters to your sponsored child. Visit them at Compassion International. com and choose a child today!

Show Hope is a movement to care for orphans all over the globe. Check out their website with your kids on your lap. Choose a way and make a way for a child's life to be forever changed.

Family Time Training is a ministry to assist you in building Biblical principals in your family's life. You can learn more by going to famtime.com

99033053R00103

Made in the USA
Lexington, KY
12 September 2018